BACK NEXT YEAR!

The Story of Following Stockport County and the 20/21 season

By Stewart Taylor

First published in Great Britain in 2021
Copyright © Stewart Taylor 2021
Published by Victor Publishing - victorpublishing.co.uk

ISBN: 9798532654327

victorpublishing.co.uk

CONTENTS

ABOUT THE AUTHOR

Stewart is married with three children and lives near Stockport He attended his first County match in 1975, aged eight with his Granddad who was a big Man United fan. Playing and watching football soon became an "obsession". After watching both United and County, the latter team took over and Stewart became a home and away Stockport loyalist. This provided a roller coaster experience as County flattered to deceive with brief moments of success.

His other hobby is music. Stewart has written a book on rock music and also contributed to magazines and fanzines reviewing rock albums and concerts.

Other interests include being a radio presenter and motorcycling. You can listen to his Classic Album Tracks Show on greatermanchesterrockradio.co.uk

FOREWORD

Stockport County Football Club have navigated a rollercoaster journey up and down the leagues. Back on the up after hitting rock bottom this book reviews the 2020/2021 season through the eyes of a supporter who attends home and away matches.

For twenty years from 1970, Stockport County had been perennial under-achievers. Often threatened with demotion to non-league football with only the re-election system saving them from anonymity. I whole generation of fans were lost to the draw of the big Manchester clubs. However, many still cherished their local team hoping for rays of football sunlight. Fortunes eventually changed.

By the 1990's County were on the up and progressed at a rapid rate that can only be described as a football miracle. The Hatters even surpassed some big rivals climbing to the edge of the play-offs to the Premier League. Then in true County fashion, the team plummeted back through the divisions into non-league football. Now, with new local owners (and County supporters) the club has some investment.

With the global pandemic, preparations for the new season provided an even greater challenge than usual for the home and away loyalist. The chapters were written in real time and preparation plans were scuppered by the ongoing pandemic. The chance to get back into grounds to watch the matches live kept being put back. However, this provided a unique perspective as the season progressed.

In another twist, the board sacked County manager and club legend Jim Gannon half-way through the season with the club in a healthy fourth place in the league table. Replaced by an unknown but highly rated youth coach that fitted a new "culture" at the club.

The season developed into a unique period in the clubs history. Read the record of the 20/21 season with a nod to the past and an eye on the future.

INTRODUCTION

Friday 25th April 1986

A cold spring evening and I am walking down Hardcastle Rd along the façade of the main stand of Edgeley Park home of Stockport County AFC. The brick walls feature large letters cast in stone spelling the name of the beleaguered club. Stockport are perennial dwellers of the bottom half of Division Four of the English Football League. Sometimes finishing in the last four places. A situation requiring re-election.

Re-election was a process where clubs had to apply to retain their league status. The old boys club of football club directors would vote for each other not to be relegated to non-league. Inevitably the likes of Rochdale, Crewe, Hartlepool and Stockport would ensure that each other were protected against the dreaded drop. This was at the expense of regular winners of non-league's top division such as Altrincham.

County are playing Tranmere, another team that played home games on a Friday night. Friday night was in theory a way of protecting attendances as both clubs operated in the shadow of two big local rivals who played on Saturday's. Everton and Liverpool in the case of Tranmere and Man Utd and City for County. This theory was open for debate as tonight's attendance is a measly 1,896. English football in the mid 80's was blighted by hooliganism and disasters such as Heysel and the Bradford City fire. Crowds were at an all-time low.

The Tranmere match is County's 3171st league game. Since winning the Fourth Division title in 1967 the club had been consistently average. Relief was only provided by the odd cup shock when the team somehow beat West Ham and

Sunderland. Or narrowly lost to Liverpool and Man Utd. The Hatters had been occupants of the basement division for nearly twenty straight years. Only Rochdale served a longer sentence. County were re-elected on four occasions and never finished above 11th since dropping back into the Fourth Division in 1970.

Born in Stockport in 1967 when County won the league, I was brought up as a Man Utd fan through my Granddad. My mate on this evening was a City fan through his Dad and we were both County sympathisers. Most County fans also followed a Manchester team. Unless you were older and could remember any semblance of success. My Granddad took me to County matches in the 70's as a small boy. On one occasion it was to see George Best play for County when George made a few appearances which boosted crowds temporarily towards the 10,000 mark.

In April '86 I had just returned from living in California for four years where my parents had moved and I was now back in Offerton, Stockport. I visited Old Trafford to see Man Utd complete an anti-climax of a season. After winning their first ten matches and potentially exorcising the ghosts of the past, the Red Devils failed to win the league again. It had been nearly twenty years since winning the First Division and in that time Utd's arch-enemies, Liverpool, had dominated. United were still the biggest club in England much to the scousers chagrin but the Reds seemed to blow up when it came to completing the job at hand – the Holy Grail.

While my Granddad was alive until 2005, support for the United cause needed to be displayed. After all, he had hardly missed a home game from 1945 until 1998 when he got too old to walk up Warwick Rd or Sir Matt Busby Way as it is now known. By '99 United had reached the Holy Grail of winning the Premier League and completed the treble.

The ultimate treble of Champions League, Premier League and FA Cup. Where were County? Unbelievably, in Division One, now the Championship or the second tier of English football. Where was I when United reached the pinnacle of the treble? I was at Edgeley Park! I certainly celebrated that amazing finish in Barcelona. However by then, I was a season ticket holding Hatter.

It is a football affair and how did the ugly duckling win out? I will tell you how in the following chapters.

I will also provide a game-by-game review of the 2020/2021 season as I "attend" home and away league and cup games played by Stockport County. Post the pandemic of spring 2020, football will take on a new challenge. As County aim for the new Holy Grail of a return to the English Football League, I will be there for every twist and turn.

CHAPTER ONE
June 2020

There are casual football fans and the obsessed. Fans that are into every statistic. The drinking fan who is too oiled to focus on the match. The ones that concentrate on all the match however good or bad. There is the singer, the non-singer, the moaner and the unflinchingly positive fan. There is the impartial observer and the biased loyalist. In fact, a football crowd contains all types to fill a Charles Darwin profiling exercise. Fortunately, evolution has developed as more women and children attend matches compared to previous decades.

Non-league clubs generally don't have issues with aggro or abusive incidents but the ex-league clubs with larger followings still have potential for it. Non-league engenders a spirit of good will between rivals. The best chants are humorous and in support of your own team.

2020 may be a watershed? We do not know exactly how and when football crowds will gather again. As of June 2020, and the pandemic, logistics will change at sports events. Football will return at some point during the 20/21 season but when the season starts and how fans are managed is still unknown.

Coupled with the Black Lives Matter movement and general examination of societal behaviour, there may be changes in crowd interaction but who knows? When the whistle blows, we will find out.

As a football fan I fall into the category of appreciating everything about the experience. From the stadiums, history, stats, attendances, kits to the live action itself. I buy in to the whole culture. Walking along Hardcastle Road in 1986 at the

Tranmere match I looked at those big painted letters on the main stand and saw architectural elegance. Most just walk past it but I tend to look at those letters spelling Stockport County AFC and appreciate the design.

The original wooden main stand burnt down in 1935 and the "new" stand mirrors the terraced streets with its brick façade. The AFC stands for Association Football Club which is a nice traditional touch. Generally, AFC was used by teams in towns with rugby league clubs such as Hull or Wigan. This was to distinguish the club apart from the Rugby Football Club. Which does not apply to Stockport now but the stadium was built for the long defunct Stockport Rugby League Club in 1901.

I will provide a virtual tour of Edgeley Park '86 as the match itself wasn't particularly interesting ending in a typical end of season 1-1 draw. Entering through pay on the gate turnstiles, probably about £2.50 at the time, we walked around the back of the goal at the Cheadle End. This end was about ten concrete steps with no roof. The previous wooden construction was demolished in 1985 because of requirements for non-wooden stands after the Bradford City fire disaster. Then around the Cheadle End onto the Popular (Pop) side to take our position on the terrace opposite the main stand.

The Pop side was halved in size in 1978 as it was falling into disrepair. There was no need for the capacity to accommodate the few loyalists that rattled around Edgeley Park. Rather inconveniently, a big gap was left between the back wall and the roof which allowed the wind to whip though and make the overall experience of watching County in the 80's even more uncomfortable.

Behind the other goal was a small open terrace called the Railway End. Edgeley is known for its large train station, a main stop on the Manchester to London line. For the Tranmere match, the wind whipped through the back of the Pop side and the game passed by without much fuss. It was another disappointing end to a season for County.

Remarkably the team flirted with the top four until form faded away resulting in a decent (for County) but ultimately disappointing eleventh place finish.

This match began my County supporting affair. Maybe it was the characterful stadium, maybe it was home-town attraction. Possibly it was the nice blue and white striped shirts or maybe it was just because they needed my support. After all, if a football fanatic like me doesn't support them, who will? There were 1,895 other masochists in the ground that night. If many more don't bother, then Stockport may lose their football team. That would be a big shame or even a tragedy. After all, we can't all be Man Utd fans.

At the time it was OK to follow little County as well as City or United. Stockport were the no-hopers who would never get out of the Fourth Division. They were more likely to drop out of the league if the swindle of re-election was taken away and relegation was introduced. There would be another few year of hurt for the Hatters but with the dawn of the 90's came a messiah and his name was Danny Bergara. Probably the most important man in the football clubs history. After joining as manager in March 1989, the team was transformed. That season was nearly over and County just survived finishing 20th. Then this happened-

89/90- 4th in Division 4 (lost in the Play-Off semi-final)

90/91- 2nd in Division 4- Promoted to Division 3

91/92- 5th in Division 3- Lost in Play-Off Final at Wembley & Lost in Autoglass Trophy Final at Wembley

92/93- 6th in new Division 2 & Lost Autoglass Trophy Final at Wembley

93/94- 4th in new Division 2- Lost in Play-Off Final at Wembley

This was a miracle turnaround in fortune for the Hatters. Not only had the club achieved promotion, but also reached Wembley an astounding four times in four years.

Unfortunately losing all the matches. Two play-off finals and two cup finals. All with a brand of entertaining football. Going toe to toe with famous clubs such as Stoke and Burnley in play-offs and cup finals. To the point that the Hatters became their main rivals in those years. From re-election battles with Hartlepool and Rochdale to finals against Stoke and Burnley almost overnight.

You had to pinch yourself if you'd watched County in the eighties. The nineties continued on an upward trend with top half finishes and then promotion in 96/97 under manager Dave Jones to Division 1 or the second tier of English football. Then an eighth-place finish in 97/98 just two places off the play-offs for the Premier League!

The local derby became Man City and we even had the temerity to beat them at Maine Road and Edgeley Park. This is when the little old County acceptance faded slightly as far as County's big brothers were concerned. Suddenly you were either a County fan or a City fan (or United) and not both at the same time. However, right-minded folk know that a lot of County fans have an affinity with City or United through family members.

I still hope United win and follow County and this is where the book now focusses. The 20/21 season as the Hatters embark on a promotion push in the National League- the top division in non-league. The prize either through automatic promotion or the play-offs is a place back in the EFL in League 2. Most football fans will agree that Stockport County are a League club. League 1 is our true home with potentially a bid for the Championship in the next 5-10 years.

CHAPTER TWO
The Challenge

The challenge is to watch the maximum amount of County games in the 20/21 season. As many as possible in the flesh and the remainder via radio, live website stream or social media. It always amazes me the lengths that some supporters go to attend all their teams matches. Actual live attendance of all matches is achieved by several hardcore supporters of most clubs. Some fanatics even go years and occasionally decades with-out missing live games. This often stretches into hundreds and even thousands of consecutive matches. In extreme examples some nutters even watch reserve or youth level matches. Some dedicate their lives to following their team. There are several key factors involved in these levels of commitment-

Relationships- missing family occasions, weddings, funerals and birthdays.

Cash- dedicating one's last funds and even lending or going into debt to cover the costs.

Work- missing out on career opportunities to remain flexible enough or even getting sacked for bunking off for that midweek away at Plymouth or Southend.

Sanity- back-to-back relegations and last-minute cup exits take a toll.

The Stockport factor- after our glorious rise to 8th in the second tier of English football, County then made the return journey back to the bottom of the bottom league just like 1986. Then in a further desperate nadir dropped even further to the second tier of non-league football. Yes, four relegations.

Conclusion- watching every game a team plays over a sustained period will send you round the bend, especially if you are a County fan.

I've done it once. The attendance of all first team matches in one season that is. That was 1999/2000. We finished seventeenth. Some great victories that season. 2-1 at Maine Rd stands out. After that December victory we only won about three games. I kept the faith though.

Why then am I going to try to attend all Stockport County first team matches of the 20/21 season?

At this point I must add, I am giving myself some wriggle room as I have reminded myself of where our away fixtures are this season. Most football fans toy with the idea of attending every game and end up falling short when reality kicks in. Usually it will be when your reasoning is called in to question by a loved one as you get your scarf out ready for a third match in a week. A final straw will break the camel's back. Maybe that Tuesday night FA Trophy trip to Dorking Wanderers followed by an away match at Torquay four days later. Then Hartlepool away the following Tuesday. Sometimes the commitment borders on madness.

Now seems like a good time as 20/21 might just be a season to remember. County are on a roll. The Hatters were National Conference North champions in 2018/19. In 2019/20 we narrowly missed out on the play-offs. Losing out to Barnet on points per game after occupying the final play-off spot due to the pandemic. The football club has a new owner- Mark Stott a local businessman and County fan. The club now has zero debt putting themselves in a strong position for a return to the Football League. The squad will go full time for the 20/21 season and quality new signings are promised.

A record of attending every game has been expertly written by Dave Espley in his book Saturday Night and Thursday Morning. Dave attended all 67 County games in 1996/97- the longest season in the club's history. That season County finished second in Division 2, gaining promotion to Division

1 (now the Championship). There were good cup runs in the FA Cup, Auto Windscreens Shield and all the way to the semi-final of the Coca Cola (League Cup). In the Coca Cola Cup run County beat Sheffield Utd, Blackburn, West Ham and Southampton. Then went out over two legs by the odd goal to Middlesbrough. Simply, the best-ever season in the history of Stockport County AFC.

Dave also edited the well-respected County fanzine The Tea Party. With the demise of printed fanzines, The Tea Party podcast (now amalgamated as the Scarf Bergara Wore) is well worth a listen. Hats off to Dave and I can only hope that 20/21 is half as good. The opposition will not be quite as salubrious but there is a feeling in my football bones, that like 96/97, something is brewing at County.

I am unlikely to match Dave's achievement of complete attendance of the seasons fixtures but I am going to give it a good go. Apart from the usual complications of life that prevent total match attendance, 20/21 has some unique challenges. Due to the pandemic fall out, it is unknown whether all matches will be available for attendance. Will the early matches be behind closed doors? Will away fans be allowed at matches? Will there be a cap on the number of fans allowed into home and away games?

I endeavour to attend as many County matches as possible home and away. Home attendance is a given (subject to the pandemic) and for away matches I can give a bit of a field trip report on each visit.

For my own entertainment on my (potential) travels I am going to set up a scoring system for the various factors and delights involved in footy journeys.

Scoring System categories –

Town- in the National League due to its level in the football pyramid there may be a fallen giant but more than likely the opposition will be from smaller towns or even provincial outposts. This makes for interesting preparation in terms of finding out exactly where some of the places are on the map. Fortunately, being 53 and having worked around the country, I've been to most of the provincial outposts already.

Pies/ culinary delights- luckily, pies are usually better the further down the leagues you go and cheaper than the corporate machines in the Premier League- so I will let you know.

The opposition fans – like pies the fans tend to be better down the leagues – more friendly and one may even buy you a pint. Unless we are at Wrexham who aren't keen on the English.

Beer- one of the best aspects of lower league grounds is the chance of quality beer. Less chance of corporate rip off Premier League £6 bottles of Heineken. More chance of some proper local ales or real ale bars such as at FC United (although they tend to forget the non-league rule of being friendly to away fans).

The Stadium- this is a very important factor to the away day follower. There will be several grounds at this level that I have not visited before and especially in the FA Trophy. They are likely to be far more characterful than the shiny new grounds up the leagues. But I better check – there are a few shiny ones down at this level too.

Memorable Moments- this could be a goal, foul, refereeing aberration, managerial meltdown, pitch invasion (by man or beast), moment of unbelievable skill, chant, mistake, blow me away pie, pint, meteorological incident, or general force majeure.

Scoring system (in points, as in 1 bad, 5 magnifico) -

1- Not very impressive at all- as in either a bit of a dump, nothing really happened in the match, fans were particularly inhospitable, food was inedible, beer was flat and weak, no roof on the away end.

2- Bog standard- things in general were bang average- could include the opposition fans chants, the pies were lukewarm, beer was just cans of Fosters etc.

3- Acceptable fare- opposition fans sing with their own original songs, pies at a minimum Hollands standard, beer on draft, there is a roof on the away end.

4- Good away day- good atmosphere, good banter with the opposition fans, good game on the pitch, County get at least a draw and the grub and beer are decent.

5- Magnifico- County win away, entertaining game, top atmosphere, great beer, great pies and no traffic jams on the way home.

If I can remember or manage to stick to the plan, I will also try to log the attendance, goals, man of the match and miles travelled. If I am smart enough, I will get one of those fuel rewards cards (I need a new hedge strimmer).

But I might just nick most of the info from the club website or social media. Writing notes on the terrace makes you look like a train spotter. That is not a great look. I won't buy the matchday programme (I find them a bit dull) but I will purchase any available fanzines (there may be one or two still out there). Fanzines tend to have a dark sense of humour which makes articles more interesting. I like old football programmes for the nostalgia. Modern era programmes feel like they have all been censored in some central football intelligence unit. To be fair, County have always had decent programmes.

I am now getting excited and just hope I can get through this. Only force majeure can stop me now. As I write, it is the middle of June 2020, so I am leaving a bit to chance with the pandemic situation. However, I am confident that by September the league will start with fans in attendance. Fingers crossed and hoping for a Danny Bergara or Dave Jones season. Come on Jim Gannon, have mercy on me.

Jim- by the way, I do need some mercy as I have just checked the potential away journeys and distances involved and it looks more challenging than presumed for the away matches. I only live three miles from Edgeley Park – so no excuses for home games.

Writing pre-playoffs, the actual list of teams is not confirmed but with-out doubt the National League will have a big Southern bias. There may be around six reasonably "local-ish" away days but the other eighteen or so destinations are miles away. Way down south or way up the northeast. Oh well, that fuel station rewards card looks like it will buy a hedge strimmer.

If anybody is reading this with an armed forces or sales back-ground they will be familiar with the military adage, the seven P's-

"Proper Planning and Preparation Prevents Piss Poor Performance."

But then again, too much preparation prevents potential partaking. Plus, if I am talking about the following twelve months, then unknown factors come in to play. One rather predictable challenge has already presented itself in the last day. An announcement that the big family Xmas do at our house has been moved from Xmas day to Boxing Day. In a rather annoying fixture change by my unsuspecting wife, I am already having to consider plans.

Boxing Day is usually a local match but will still take a minimum two and a half hours to complete. If at home on a Boxing Day, it will take me approximately fifteen minutes to drive the three miles to the ground. Plus a two-minute jog from the car to the ground (I am an expert on good parking locations). A five-minute entry into the stand. Plus stoppages by the ref etc. Minimum two and a half hours out of the middle of the day. If it is an away match, then I am not even going to calculate the time challenge.

I do have sympathy with Premier League fans who deal with several different kick off scenarios and TV re-arrangements. At least I know that when the fixture list comes out County will play all their matches at the time and date on the list. That is 3pm on Saturday for most of them so I know where I stand. Accepting the possibility of force majeure of course.

First challenge – Xmas dinner fixture re-arrangement back to its rightful place – Xmas Day. It is a no-brainer really. The reason for this fixture change is the construction of an all singing, all dancing summer house. Sounds posher than it is. A construction in the garden that will house a bigger than normal gathering of folk and will double up as the grand opening of the structure. With some invitees doing other stuff on Xmas Day, the thought is that Boxing Day is a good option.

I must say at this point, that I have not declared the extent of my football attendances in this forthcoming season. The wife is used to my absence on most Saturday's. She has got quite used to it over the last twenty odd years. However, this time there will be a few extra games to say the least.

I did once take my lovely wife to a match. It was Walsall at home in the early 2000's and as we sat in the Cheadle End a storm ensued. For fifteen minutes we watched the advertising hoardings being uprooted and dumped in the Railway End goal mouth. I had never seen anything like it and this extended the game by a good twenty minutes as the boards were collected and strapped down. To say the least, she was glad to get back home after an extended period of boredom. Of course, I was quite used to enduring long periods of the mundane before being rewarded with fleeting moments of football elation.

I will update you on the outcome of this fixture pile-up. It is only June and there are already fixture issues!

Word count update- I am around the 4000-word mark. I haven't done any travel prep yet and I am running headlong into this "book". The fixture list is not out, so specific dates and locations are not available. However, I do need to consider other factors than just me and Stockport County 20/21.

Daughter – in Uni. Pretty much self-sufficient. I am on call for any assistance but if I always carry the fixture list with me, I can ensure no "fixture" clashes.

Son 1- starting Uni somewhere around September / October or whenever the pandemic dictates. Pretty much self-sufficient (carry fixture list to ensure no fixture clashes).

Son 2- will be in year 11- pretty much self-sufficient. Need to consider the matches he plays in, but they are usually on a Sunday and he will be coming to County with me (should not be a problem).

Birthday's- check all relatives birthdays against the fixture list to anticipate potential fixture clashes and come up with an action plan (in case somebody organises something where I am expected to be in attendance).

School holidays -check all term times to anticipate any family trips against the fixture list and come up with an action plan.

Booking a Holiday - monitor any activity by the wife that looks like holiday website searching and general conversations with others that sound like going away during the football season etc.

OK, I feel a bit selfish, but this is likely to be a one-off season. I have set myself the challenge and I am determined to achieve the goal (of as many matches as poss). Hopefully, there will be more goals by County in more matches than the opposition to make this whole darn thing worthwhile!

Now, when to tell the missus? Probably need to wait to find out when the season is going to start with all this pandemic situation. I suppose there are several factors that could affect this plan working including-

When will the season start?

Will it even start?

When will it end?

Will fans be allowed in to all the matches? (this could scupper my objective)

If a match takes place without fans, is there any way to be in the stadium?

How do I get a press pass? (this may enable me entry to a lock down stadium)

Can I volunteer at County? (this may enable entry to a lock down stadium)

Then there is the "force majeure" strategy. If there is no resolution to entry to a stadium, do I just sneak in. After all, several of the grounds in this league are quite small with easy access over a small wall or gate. Or possibly an "incognito" strategy. Through my work I have a full set of PPE (personal protection equipment). This includes high-viz jacket, gloves, and goggles. I could pretend to be a steward or groundsman.

PS- I have now told the missus. She is OK with it. Well, the general concept of watching all the homes games and a lot of away games. I have also mentioned that most of the away games are at the other end of the country. I think this has registered. However, I have not had the balls (yet) to mention or address the Boxing Day fixture clash.

CHAPTER THREE
Logistics, Preparation, Reality Check

June 2020

This chapter covers potential away days, favourites places to sit in Edgeley Park, the joy of watching County and some of my favourite County kits. An introduction of sorts to pre-season and the upcoming league campaign.

It is official now. County have been replaced by Barnet in the play-offs on the points per game basis. Barnet are currently eleventh and County reside in the last play-off place in seventh. Barnet have four games in hand but are only four points behind us. We are top of the form table so there is some injustice. Barnet get through for having a crap pitch which meant they have accrued games in hand. Barnet conveniently postponed some matches earlier in the season due to the inadequate drainage of rainwater. Something to do with preparing for a cup match if I recall correctly. Anyway, the points per game formula predicted that they would have finished above us.

I am not bitter (honest). The fixtures could have been completed with more support from the football authorities. The EFL or even Premier League could have helped the football pyramid with coronavirus testing. Lower league clubs depend on revenue through the turnstiles and could not afford to do the testing and were forced to furlough players and staff.

One month's wages of a couple of top Premier League players would cover the cost of testing to fulfil the National Leagues fixtures behind closed doors. The fixtures could have been delayed slightly to lessen the impact of bringing back furloughed players. Then the true play-off teams would have been confirmed. I suppose a bit of imagination and charitable thinking from multi-millionaires is out of the question.

I am not bitter (honest).

I await the play-off results to confirm the full list of places to visit next season. As mentioned earlier there is a Southern bias in this league. Now I am in preparation mode, I may as well start to check out what this challenge entails. Before I start to regale my tale of distances, I do understand that fans of other clubs are less conveniently placed than Stockport. It goes without saying that everywhere is north of Plymouth and everywhere is south of Newcastle. I doff my cap to the super-distances that some fans travel to their away games. However, once I explain my prospective away match journeys, I am sure I will garner some sympathy.

Maybe I should have waited for another season when there are a majority of northern and midlands teams. However, embracing reality, this is a list of teams that could be visited. Rough location noted. Approximate travelling distance logged. These mileages are one way. Don't forget to double the number for the round trip!

Barnet- North London- 190 miles

Solihull Moors- South Birmingham- 100 miles

Hartlepool- Northeast- 135 miles

Woking- Southwest of London- 210 miles

Dover- Near France- 295 miles!

Bromley- South London- 235 miles

Sutton- Southwest London- 222 miles

Torquay- Near France- 260 miles!!

Aldershot- Hampshire- 220 miles

Eastleigh- Somewhere near the south coast- 220 miles

Dagenham- East London- 220 miles (again)!!!

I think Chesterfield and Wrexham are still in but it looks like Chorley are down. Halifax might be in for some local travelling relief!!

This may require some imagination-

A trip to the English Riviera (Torquay) with the missus? Hopefully while the weather is still Riviera-ish. Trip to France with the Dover match on the way? "Fancy a trip to London love?" Take your pick- Sutton, Dagenham, Bromley, Barnet, Wealdstone. How about another trip to France from Portsmouth (via Eastleigh or the Aldershot match)?

Ideally, I need to somehow recruit the missus. Maybe if County are winning every week the prospect may be more attractive. Something to work on.

Logistics for the home games at Edgeley Park-

Fans have an affinity with their football ground. At County we are lucky that we have a ground that has retained some of its character. The reason for this, is that it is old. New shiny stadiums are bland and functional. Edgeley Park is old.

There is a good chance that I will attend some of the games on my own this season. Especially the away games. I will see and meet regulars at the match itself, but my County sympathiser friends and family are less bonkers than me. They will attend "if they feel like it" on the day. Plus, it won't be easy to get recruits for a Tuesday night game in Eastleigh (Eastleigh is somewhere near Southampton).

This is good though, as I am in writing mode so will get in the zone of observer. The solo traveller focussed on chronicling the rise of Stockport County. Like a phoenix from the ashes.

My 16-year-old son is a recruit especially if County are smashing it at the top of the league (otherwise he may find excuses to avoid the pain). My older son will potentially go on his return visits from Uni. Two doors down on my street are County fans. I have a mate who is so football mad he will be a willing accomplice (but it depends how County are doing- there is only so much pain you can inflict on a mate).

Season tickets needs to be purchased. Over the years I have sat/ stood in most of the ground. Starting on the Pop Side standing, Railway End standing, Cheadle End seats and Pop Stand seats.

This brings me to the 7 P's of marketing: Product, Price, Promotion, Packaging, Positioning and People. With our new owners undoubtedly beavering away enthusiastically across the board room table in preparation for our return to the football league, I am sure the 7 P's are at the forefront.

We have already seen great progress in social media plus-

Product- well, let's see what happens, but going full-time and bringing new players in will help.

Price- tickets frozen for a few years and a forecast of an improved team.

Packaging- new kits look smart and we have a new badge.

Positioning- well, we were in a play-off position until Barnet sabotaged their own pitch in anticipation of points per game. Seriously though, we are well positioned for a promotion push.

There you go, I am a marketing manager!

So, where shall I sit?

The Cheadle End

Built in about '95 and the brainchild of chairman Brendan Ellwood and his board, this towers over Edgeley Park and holds about 5,000 people or roughly half the capacity of the ground. The singers are in the smaller upper tier. If County are playing well and the bottom tier joins in the chanting, the Cheadle End creates an impressive din.

Brendan should have done two smaller stands with one at the Railway End. This was the beginning of the end for Mr Ellwood as he began to have delusion of grandeur eventually losing touch with the fans. About five years later he thought that a name change to ManStock County and a move to Maine Rd (while profiteering from the sale of Edgeley Park) might be a good idea. This was when Man City were preparing to move to Eastland's.

Fortunately, Manchester City Council gave permission for use of Maine Road to Sale Sharks instead. In a bizarre twist of fate Brendan sold County to Brian Kennedy, owner of Sale Sharks. Sale did not move into Maine Rd. They waited until they owned Edgeley. Wow, this is ripe for a conspiracy theory. We became tenants to the egg-chasers and a slow and painful demise took place for County (with the odd bright spot such as Wembley 2008).

At several points since the Sale debacle I was convinced we were going bust. I didn't get into the details and preferred to just watch nervously from the side lines. However, there was sterling work by fan groups over the years to keep the club alive.

Popular (Pop) Side (Vernon Stand, Barlow and now Together Stand)

This was the main standing and singing area until the new Cheadle End was built and seats were put in the Pop side. This had a great atmosphere especially in the early 90's when County were on the up. There are still a few vocal Pop Side loyalists on the halfway line and the banter with the opposition fans housed on the other side of the halfway line is good. If the weather is nice, County (sometimes known as the friendly club) let the away fans on the Railway End but generally they are housed on the Pop Side.

The Railway End

An open terrace but with seats bolted on the steps. The worst kind of seats. Firstly, the leg room is probably crap and secondly as this ground is situated in the northwest of England it rains a lot. Its occupants get very wet. County have mercy on most away fans and put them in the Pop side. But if we do play Burnley, Stoke or City there will be no resistance from County fans in housing said peeps in this area.

NB- to be honest, for any County fans under the age of 40 this Burnley, Stoke, City reference probably does not resonate much. But for old gits like me with long memories it comes naturally! Oh yeah, might as well add Peterborough and Port Vale to the list. For any younger readers, those two teams beat us at Wembley in the early 90's. Four Wembley losses on the bounce so they can go on the rainy Railway End as well.

The Main Stand (The Danny Bergara Stand)

The executive area is also in the Main Stand which features a small walled off section and some padded seats. There are no executive boxes (just in case you may have expected anything fancy). The main entertaining is done in the Cheadle End executive suits in the bowels of said edifice.

Being entertained in the Cheadle End can result in a touch of barracking if you are a celebrity. On one occasion I sat near Coronation Streets Les Battersby, the City supporting B list celebrity, in the Cheadle End as County proceeded to beat City (again). To be fair, Les took our cajoling quite well and I have liked him ever since.

There we have it. It will be back in the Pop side for us. Good side on view and good banter on the halfway line.

On several occasions I have over-sold the idea of a visit to Edgeley Park to unsuspecting mates and family members. These of course are not hardcore County fans and the prospect of future attendance versus watching City and United live or on TV is a no contest. I've usually got them back for one or two games, but I have not managed many religious conversions.

There was one match where I thought I was on to something. We played Carlisle in 2006 on the final day of the season and we needed a draw to stay in the football league (which we got). Therefore, avoiding the nadir of a drop into non-league football. We did of course achieve that nadir eventually. For the Carlisle match I managed to cajole some sympathisers on the basis that it was their civic duty with the fact that they were Stopfordians. Or had a tenuous link to the town and therefore they must support their local team in their hour of need.

On this occasion I didn't over-sell the experience as the match was an emotional atmosphere, the ground was full –

over 10,000. There was also a friendly pitch invasion at the end and the atmosphere was probably completely different compared to the corporate Premier League. The following season, one mate who was there even started going to a few matches. Until he came up with an excuse. Something to do with "I would rather walk round B & Q with the missus than watch that crap". Bit harsh I thought.

The Joy of County

There have been times when I feel I have inflicted some peer pressure on my sons into the charms of County and then failed spectacularly with the end product. Of course, United has some added attractions I suppose. One result I have had is that my youngest sons favourite kit is the 2008 County classic when the Hatters beat Rochdale at Wembley in the play-off final. Also, he really liked the Carlton Palmer era home shirt. That is two results in my eyes. My eldest son didn't take much interest in County. Even at an early age he had already sussed out that getting any connection with County would be counter-productive to his mental health and stuck with United.

My brother just thought the County thing was because I was a football fanatic and would watch any match that happened to be taking place. Which is probably true. I have watched Salisbury, St Mirren, Droylsden, Altrincham, Notts County and many more just because I was working near the ground or someone wanted to go. Also, on return from the States in '86 and being old enough to travel to games, I visited loads of grounds. Most stadiums were still in their original classic "state" then. I probably visited half the 92 league grounds just to check them out.

County certainly did get dismissed a bit by local football fans. With all my family and most mates being either City or United anything other than the big two was off the radar. Everyone was cool with the idea of County though. My Granddad was blunt as he was hardcore United and just referred to County as crap. I think it was a statement of fact in his mind rather than any dislike. He was from before political correctness. With his generation you got a succinct and honest response. The best way.

After all, County were indeed crap on many occasions and more than likely when I attended a County matches with him in the 70's. I was too young to probably notice.

There are advantages with County though compared to City or United-

• Anybody at County is there because they really, really want to be there for County (apart from possibly some free ticket attendees and people there for the food and booze on a jolly in the executive suite).

• The fans are almost exclusively local and true County fans (rather than day-trippers, tourists and prawn sandwich eaters- which now applies to City as well as United).

• Any victory is a victory rather than a formality (City and United have been so good, that a home win has become a formality).

• It is affordable and you can always get away tickets (following United and City home and away in recent times has become a very expensive operation to get away tickets unless you go to all the matches and spend your life savings on the cause).

• On the last point, I would add that the loyalty and lengths that some United and City fans go to procuring away tickets and travel in Europe is amazing. So, they are not included in the prawn sandwich brigade.

• Watching lower league football is more fun, self-deprecating and humorous than the Prem (which has become a bit self-obsessed and too serious).

• It is affordable and you can take others who can sit next to you (at Prem grounds you cannot just attend a game with mates and sit together unless you have the use of season tickets together)

I would say a complete justification for swapping the Etihad or Old Trafford for Edgeley Park. Go on, you know you want to!

Of course, at this stage (June 20) we don't have a clear idea of when we will be able to attend matches at Edgeley Park, The Etihad or Old Trafford. As I write, the first match after lockdown is about to take place. Man City v Arsenal at the Etihad which will be empty- literally. Apart from a reported maximum 300 people. That is both squads, management, back-room staff, match officials and whoever is required to open-up a stadium safely and manage the match. Plus, Mike Summerbee (he is always there) and Brian Kidd who is employed by City but nobody is quite sure what he does. Plus, Les Battersby or a cardboard cut-out version.

There are rumours of piped in crowd noise which has worked quite well in the Bundesliga apparently. Or the option of just the sound of the players. I experienced something similar watching County in the 80's. Back then there was no problem with social distancing and you could hear the tea lady boiling the kettle in the changing rooms just before half time. Unless County scored of course. Then there would be shocked cheers or mild profanity from fans who missed the goal as they were talking to their mates and not watching the match.

I was distracted by dogs on the Pop side. I remember one bloke used to bring his dog on. I doubt he paid admission but at least it boosted the attendance. Great days indeed. After the arrival of Danny Bergara, the Pop side was transformed from a sparsely populated area to a packed terrace with everyone watching the match.

Returning to City v Arsenal behind closed doors. In Germany they had thousands of cardboard cut-outs of fans. Bit boring really. It would be far more interesting if City deployed cardboard cut outs of their celebrity fans. Maybe Helen the Bell, Curly Watts, Little and Large, Bernard Manning and Les Battersby of course.

County would have a far cooler cardboard cut-out crowd. Blossoms (famous local band), The Still (great local band and highly recommended for any weddings and dos), Oliver Holt (well-known journo), Tony O'Shea (darts player), Daz Sampson (the singer) and of course Mike Yarwood RIP.

The Kit

If I can write about cardboard cut-out fans, I can write about football kits. The kit was invented to distinguish sporting teams from each other. In the heat of battle and covered in mud (before the inception of geo-technology grass that you get at the Etihad or Old Trafford). We play on real grass at Edgeley Park and in the winter you get muddy.

The point of a kit was to make you contrast the opposition (this later had the added benefit of giving viewers some way of distinguishing between teams on black and white telly). The kit was plain and functional. This trend carried on for nigh on a hundred years until the replica kit was born.

Manufacturers such as Admiral and Umbro went design crazy somewhere in the mid 1970's. Before that, kits were a magnificent template of cotton. Simple and affective. Red, white cuffs and collar- you could have been Man Utd, Swindon or Crewe. Royal Blue, white cuffs and collar- Everton, Gillingham or Chesterfield. Then Admiral and Umbro etc started to introduce their logo's down the sleeves and the replica kit was born.

Here are my top 5 County kits of all time -

1. The 1979 to 82 Mike Summerbee Argentina kit.

The Adidas sky blue and white stripes, black shorts affair was an Argentina kit. A replica 1978 World Cup kit supplied by Adidas who had a base in the borough. New manager Mike Summerbee took on the job as player-manager partly as he lived locally. We needed a new kit for the 79/80 season.

With Mike being a famous footballer, friend of George Best and mover and shaker on the Manchester night life scene he was well connected. One associate was Adi Dassler. Adi was one half of the brotherly German inventors of Adidas. Mike called on Adidas for a favour and procured a load of kit on which the County badge was added.

The result: County were the best dressed football team in the Fourth Division. Plus, this shirt is number 20 of the top 50 shirts of all time according to Four-Four-Two magazine! The kit had to be changed in January 82 as the Falklands war got in the way and it was deemed inappropriate to wear the Argentina kit. It was replaced just after Xmas with a black and white off the shelf number. Sacrilege!

2. The orange and black Andy Kilner-era away kit

This was the kit when we beat City 2-1 at Maine Road in December '99. This away kit is immortalised in this victory as County beat their big brother to move into the play-off positions and within touching distance of the Premier League. Andy Kilner was manager, the County fans revelled in victory and the City fans got really pissed off and chased County fans all around Rusholme after the match. Times have changed since then and it is unlikely that our paths shall cross again. But just as an excuse to revel in the County v City results from that era here you go: Won 3, Drew 2, Lost 1. Not Bad.

Stockport County - Manchester City		2:1
Manchester City - Stockport County		2:2
Stockport County - Manchester City		2:2
Manchester City - Stockport County		1:2
Manchester City - Stockport County		4:1
Stockport County - Manchester City		3:1

3. The Man Utd Old Trafford '78 League Cup match kit by Bukta

This kit is the one County wore for their League Cup game in front of 41,000 people. It is known for this match in which County were robbed of a famous victory by the referee. Gordon McQueen was sent off for scything down Derek Loadwick. United got a jammy free kick that was deflected into the net and then came from behind with a last minute and highly dubious penalty. Reports noted that Loadwick weaved passed McQueen and left him for dead. Loadwick cleaned McQueen's boots as a schoolboy when they were both at Leeds. The big Scot objected to his ex-teammates show boating and took Loadwick out at the knees. Summerbee also sat on the ball at one point which as an ex-City player must have wound up United. The kit itself is a classic white shirt/ blue shorts with Bukta badges down the sleeves.

This was the first County replica shirt I ever saw at Harrison's Sports in Edgeley. I was not at the game but Terry Park scored a breath-taking individual effort according to newspaper reports. Folklore had him starting a run in his own half before a mazy Maradona style dribble was converted past Gary Bailey in the United net. The game was not televised but years later footage was uncovered. A County director had taken some personal video footage which eventually made it onto a County DVD.

4. 2008 Wembley Play-off shirt

The Hatters went through a dire period in the early 2000's. When you go up the leagues you are surfing on the crest of a wave. When we were in the second tier it became clear that you need 15,000 plus crowds to survive. Unfair financial pressures kicks in. County had one good season, a couple of average campaigns and one completely disastrous season. From there it was almost completely down-hill until 2007/2008. Except for nine wins in a row without conceding a goal in 2006/2007. In 2008 County beat Rochdale 3-2 in the play-off final to return to League 1. The shirt was blue with a white horizontal band on the chest. Supplemented by subtle gold piping. The kit was one of my favourites and County were back on the up (in theory).

5. The psychedelic Robbie's bitter shirt of 93/94

Also known as the Kevin Francis shirt. Big Kev epitomised the Danny Bergara era as County started to score goals, terrorise opposition defences and appear four times at Wembley in four years. Big Kev was 6ft 7in. A nightmare for defenders and deceptively skilful. Super Kev scored more than 30 goals two seasons running and became a folk hero. The shirt in 93/94 perfectly epitomised the team and Kev. Bright and a bit flash. There was a tendency for garish patterned designs at the time and this County shirt is a perfect example of mid 90's footy couture. Consisting of fading horizontal blue and white stripes overlaid with red zigzags it somehow worked. It reminds me of some John Squire art creation knocked up for a Stone Roses record cover. With the white shorts and socks it somehow worked for me. A County classic.

CHAPTER FOUR
Decision Day

This is a day that came as no surprise (17/6/20). The National League have voted for the points per game outcome which means that County drop one place from seventh to eighth. All the 24 teams have voted and a majority have opted for this outcome. No more matches for the teams not in the play-offs. There is a points per game formula which means that Barnet have usurped us having played four games less.

They are in eleventh compared to our seventh but the computer has predicted how the remaining results pan out or the average points expected to be gained by each club. Barnet have a dodgy pitch and this is why they have played less games as the grass would not drain when it rained. Fundamental pitch failure resulting in unjustified points per game calculation.

To be honest, after a coat of thinking about it, I am not too gutted. If we were in the play-offs the whole exercise would be behind closed doors. No fans, no real celebration. It may be much sweeter to just get promoted next season with the fans in attendance. You can't beat a bit of optimism for next season on my behalf. We should be one of the strongest sides in the division and with a fair wind behind us will be in a play-off spot come next April (or whenever next season concludes).

What are the permutations of these developments?

Barrow – promoted as champions into League 2

Relegated – Fylde and Chorley (that is two local away matches gone)

Promoted into the National League- Kings Lynn (National League North champs) and Wealdstone (National League South champs).

Another trip to London for Wealdstone. I may have to calculate if it would be easier to just move to London. It would be a good location to attend nearly half of County's matches next season!

NB- at least we get the "opportunity" to bump into the Wealdstone Raider, well-known for the now infamous "You want some? I'll give it ya" threat to Whitehawk supporters. Real name Gordon Hill (not the tricky Man Utd winger from the 70's), this chap is also known for his "You've got no fans" jibe. Whitehawk, admit they haven't got many fans but County do have a few. I am quite looking forward to meeting the bard of Wealdstone and debating said topic.

PS- If you are wondering where Whitehawk FC are from (I was, so I looked it up), it is Brighton. We will probably get them in the FA Trophy. Another long-distance journey (said with a beleaguered expression)!

To compound the mounting mileage required to cover these away jaunts in the next campaign, Kings Lynn won the National League North. I had to check and as I thought, Kings Lynn is somewhere between Peterborough, Norwich and Cambridge. If I had to choose a season in which the maximum possible distances are required to follow County away, this must be the one. In any division, in any year, in the history of Stockport County AFC.

To add these two fixtures to my earlier list of long-distance treks, here we go-

(I cannot be arsed working out the permutations of who may remain in the division from the play-off spots. It is not going to make that much difference to this high mileage challenge).

Wealdstone- somewhere near/in London- 190 miles

Kings Lynn- somewhere in the Bermuda triangle (Cambridge, Peterborough and Norwich)- 145 miles

I thought Kings Lynn was more mileage but there is no comfort in those 145 miles. It is one of those slow cross-country treks to the East of England on mainly A and B roads.

County manager Jim Gannon has made an impressive announcement on social media. A nice rallying cry to the fans, team and club. The message is to "go again" next season and complete the job of promotion back to the football league. As you would expect and there is a general sense of optimism and excitement, especially with the new owners at the helm.

Football returned to our screens this week. No fans and piped in crowd noise but apart from that nothing has changed on the pitch. Villa and Sheffield United bore the audience with a 0-0 stalemate. The most exciting moment being when VAR ruled out a goal that was a good three feet over the line. In fact, the Villa goalie was nearly in the back of the net when he cleared the ball. Quite how this modern electronic equipment allowed this is anybody's guess but this magic machinery needs a good calibration. In fact, if I were the official calibrator of said machine, I would keep a low profile.

The linesman, referee, both sets of players, officials and anyone else in the stadium (there are about 300 in attendance for lockdown football), could see it was a goal. But hey, in this modern age no one wants to make a decision or stick their neck out and do what is right. The Sheffield United manager was not best pleased claiming the Villa keeper was halfway up the Holte End when he repelled the ball. Slight exaggeration as the netting itself restrained the keeper from falling over the advertising hoardings and into the Holte End.

Over at the Etihad which literally is the Emptihad on this occasion, City easily beat the Arsenal. Interestingly there were several virtual City fans in attendance. At each end of the ground there were screens showing a zoom with fans watching at home from their living rooms, kitchens and bedrooms. A little bit creepy for me. Frustratingly a lot of these fans will have been watching from their residencies within the borough of Stockport. I would just like to remind these folk that Stockport does indeed have its own team and they are called Stockport County. There is no excuse for watching world class football at the Etihad when they have a top non-league team in their own town. Rather than watch the football elegance of Kevin de Bruyne, they should be consulting their road atlases to establish the best route to Dover, Eastleigh and Kings Lynn for next season.

As for the football at the Etihad, City again proved what a magnificent football team they are. While Arsenal again proved that they are as the table shows a seventh or eighth place team. Arsenal's woes were compounded by another appearance by Sideshow Bob. Or David Luiz as he is also known. Arsenal manager Mikel Arteta had publicly stated how important Luiz is to the squad pre-match. Rather embarrassingly for both fellas, Luiz came on as a sub and proceeded to sabotage Arsenals slim chances of getting any points from the match. In 25 minutes of madness he was at fault for both of City's goals (one an embarrassing assist off his thigh as he put Sterling through). Sideshow also conceded a penalty and got sent off for a trade-mark rash challenge. Sorry David but it was a rather amusing catalogue of errors (unless you are an Arsenal fan).

CHAPTER FIVE
The Summer Diary 2020

21st June 2020

Most County fans are now settled on going again in the National League. Barnet are in the play-offs leapfrogging us on points per game.

We could have had a chance of promotion to the football league under normal circumstances but good luck to Barnet I suppose.

Now the dust has settled County are in better shape than Barnet moving forward. Barnet need a new pitch and had to lay off staff at the start of lockdown. Hopefully, that was down to financial necessity rather than convenience. County on the other hand have zero debt, have retained their staff and donated £75,000 to the NHS.

I watched Match of the Day and the Brighton v Arsenal game. I recalled that we beat Brighton away 4-2 only about ten years ago. You never know in football. Fortunes can change relatively quickly as demonstrated by Brighton and their current Premier League status and great new stadium. They beat Arsenal 2-1.

I made contact with a Japanese County fan that visited Edgeley Park earlier in the year. Often clubs attract fans from afar that tend to be quite fanatical. Akito Aoki from Tokyo has supported County for nine years after discovering The Hatters through playing the FIFA video games.

Akito decided to book a flight for the Bromley home game earlier in the season. Then storm Dennis struck and almost scuppered his ambition of watching County at EP. Fortunately the game went ahead and Akito visited several watering holes around Edgeley meeting County fans.

22nd June 2020

I have just caught up on confirmation of who will be relegated from League Two into the National League for next season. It is Stevenage. It could have been Macclesfield which would have provided a much-needed local away game and a genuine Cheshire derby. Macc have been in dire financial straits recently as the result of a dodgy owner. They have been deducted points for various rule breaking such as not paying the staff and players. This led to postponements of matches earlier in the season. They recently had more points deducted but fortunately for them they have been deferred meaning that they retain their League 2 status.

NB- Stevenage have had a reprieve and the EFL have sent Macc down instead- read more later! But I'll leave the next two paragraphs in as a reflection on how having Macc back is good!

I have noticed how Northern biased League Two is which will be a relief if County go up next season. This compares favourably with the National League which is almost like a Southern League. To compound this, Macclesfield's lucky escape means we have another southern team in Stevenage as an added long distance away day. From Hertfordshire, they are at least slightly more northernly than the London trips. Just to confirm-

Stevenage – somewhere north of London but still 177 miles!

I would still sooner be County than Macc though. Although they currently reside in the division above the Hatters, they are a natural National League side and struggle to attract more than 2000 regulars and probably more like 1500 if they were in the National League. They seemed to claim a bit of rivalry with County but we are not really that bothered about Macc. The only event that annoyed me was the 0-6 debacle we suffered at Moss Rose about 15 years ago but we were down to ten men after fifteen minutes. Good luck to them.

But spare a thought for Hartlepool. If this "southern" league seems bad for us then it is even worse for them. Spare a thought for Dover too. They are completely out on a limb, closer to France than any of their opponents and have some monster trips.

23rd June 2020

At City v Burnley some so-called Clarets supporters hired a plane to fly a banner reading "white lives matter Burnley!" Flown over the Etihad just as the players all "took a knee" in support of Black Lives Matter. The Black Lives Matter movement is in support of new ways of policing in America after the death of another black man in police "custody". The movement then developed into a campaign for overall improvements in the treatment of black people in America and across the world. This undoubtedly is a relevant movement.

The movement does not mean white lives don't matter. The "Burnley" banner was crass. However, I think the BLM support should be a respectful but temporary demonstration in football. One month would be appropriate. These things tend to get complicated when sport mixes with politics. I try to avoid politics but whoever organised the banner can only be described naïve.

26th June 2020

Liverpool have won the league. The first time in thirty years. I haven't really got much more to say about that. Oh, go on then, being semi-intelligent and the magnanimous type I will make comment. Well done. Any team that is twenty odd points ahead of the second-place team is clearly a very good side. Inevitably, their fans celebrated outside the ground in their thousands with no social distancing hugging each other en masse. Meanwhile, half a million people packed on to Bournemouth beach in the heat wave. It looks like life is back to normal for most now.

Pubs are open in a couple of weeks and we just hope there isn't a spike in infections. I have worked throughout the lockdown and the roads were almost empty in April. Now the traffic is back. From a surreal post-apocalyptic emptiness to complete crowds in the last month. The R rate is still at 1 though! Most of these "revellers" probably complained about Dominic Cummings and wanted him sacked a month ago. Humans: we have either got very short memories or are not very intelligent. Or both.

I just hope this does not affect the start of the new season. There are a couple of scenario's being put forward for the return of crowds to stadiums. One is that 25% of the ground capacity will be the maximum. At County that would be approx. 2,500. County have 2,000 season ticket holders so it is a feasible option. The big question to be answered is whether away fans will be allowed in. Another option is no fans. Ouch. Or hopefully 50%. County's average attendance will be around 50% of the capacity. Fingers crossed then.

If there are no fans allowed in grounds then this book might be quite short. Unless it becomes a cyber review as the matches are watched via the County website. I am now thinking of the best ways to accrue a press pass to gain entry into the stadium as one of the three hundred maximum attendees. Well three hundred to be confirmed. That is the figure for the Premier League and presumably allowable for any professional football match. After all, County will be full time professional next year moving up from our semi-professional status in recent years.

1st July 2020

County are back in full training today under current FA guidelines. I've discovered a book about County that I didn't own. Being a super-enthusiast albeit not a complete "anorak" this is quite exciting. In the post arrived a book called Vintage Port by Trevor Baxter an ex-reporter for the Manchester Evening News. I have several County books, videos and DVD's. I've got pretty much everything that has come to my attention. Plus, loads of match day programmes but nothing is in one place or in alphabetical order.

Being a music vinyl junky, I have copious amounts of rock stuff that would probably make a collector drool. None of it is in any order but I have a whole lot of stuff. Or a Whole Lot of Rosie as AC/DC once said. I certainly would not qualify as an anorak to the true anoraks. I would be thrown out of the club for serious non- conformity.

Vintage Port is a great review of the 96/97 season. In Trevor's book he admitted to being a United fan initially before the charms of Stockport embedded in his football soul. Like me, he attended some County matches as a youngster and then with his mates started to do the Friday night County/ Saturday afternoon big team addiction.

Trevor produced more of a pictorial review of the season compared to Dave Espley's book about the same year. I enjoyed both and Vintage Port is a welcome addition to my County "library". Trevor missed a few games in this classic season due to his other reporting commitments. I will likely follow the same trend as I placate the family post pandemic with some holiday time and family commitments. Also, having a job that has become more demanding with furlough, reduced staff and redundancies, there is a reality to my ability to attend every game of the forthcoming campaign.

However, I am determined to attend every available match. If I can attend a County match outside any essential other commitment, I will be there. So, Dover or Eastleigh away on a Tuesday night is in the diary if there are no clashes.

6th July 2020

Jim Gannon, County manager, is officially back off furlough today. The players started training last week. Now our manager is back at the helm, the much-anticipated signings should take shape. Two players have already left. Eliot Osbourne joined Stevenage and highly rated Festus Arthur has joined Championship club Hull City. Good news is we will get cash for Festus. Probably somewhere between 40k and 100k plus add-ons depending on appearances etc.

It feels like we are letting some leave but there are better players ready to take their place.

Apparently, the club is in advanced stages of negotiation with prospective talent. I have heard that one before without anything exciting happening. However, there is an increased sense of optimism these days.

I did get a bit of publishing news this week. I had a verbal offer to publish this book based on the synopsis and a sample of the early chapters. A local publisher was keen to progress the "project" to add to local Stockport area themed writings. Unfortunately, as this was muted several months ago, force majeure has indeed intervened.

A rather apologetic lady contacted me to say that due to the pandemic they have decided to limit their projects this year. A factor being the closure of some book shops in the local area which is deemed to be the main catchment area for this type of book. Also, their plan to go exclusively on-line. So a polite rejection and realistic of course.

A Stockport County book does indeed have a limited audience and low if any profit potential for a publisher. It looks like this will be self-published which I was kind of planning for anyway. I have sent a submission to a selection of smaller football focussed publishers to see what reaction it gets. I am checking my in box in anticipation but not getting over excited.

17th July 2020

Good couple of days for incoming transfers. Today Mark Kitching arrived from Hartlepool. An attacking left back with plenty of experience playing around 80 games at this level and originally a product of the Middlesbrough youth system. According to Pools fans on twitter, Mark is better going forward than defending and they were sorry to see him depart. Sounds decent.

This week saw the arrival of the Jennings brothers. Local lads and good additions to the squad. Striker Connor is familiar to Hatters fans after making sixteen loan appearances for County in the 2012/13 season scoring eight goals. The striker was on loan from Stalybridge Celtic before moving on to Tranmere making 140 appearances and featuring in promotions and Wembley play-off finals. Therefore, decent experience. Older brother James is a product of the Man City youth system. A defender, James has played for several National League and League Two teams. Most recently James was at Wrexham making 107 appearances.

Ben Hinchliffe, Ash Palmer, Sam Minihan, Jordan Keane, Adam Thomas and Nyal Bell have all signed to new full-time contracts. Paul Turnbull and Sam Walker left the club following the expiration of their contracts. Both being great servants in recent times. Paul was County's youngest ever player and captain in the National League North championship winning season. Sam was players player of the year in 2018/19. Both will be missed but it is testament to recent progress at County. We are moving forward and looking to improve the playing squad ready to challenge for the title next season. I would probably settle for play-offs but let's aim higher Hatters fans.

It is all sounding promising with the team going full-time and new additions to the squad joining. All we need now is a start date for the season and season tickets to go on sale. Fingers crossed; we are looking at a September start with fans in the ground.

18th July 2020

Boris our PM has decided that football crowds will go back in October. Which is positive as this is the first news on fans attending matches. The plan is to trial fan movement into stadiums at Charlton Athletic and Cambridge United. This is an EFL trial, so does not include the Premier League or the National League where County play.

I presume they have chosen The Valley at Charlton as a typical Championship ground with an all-seater capacity of 27,000. More interestingly for a County fan, I checked the

Abbey stadium capacity, home of Cambridge. The Abbey has a capacity of 8,127 (4,327 seated). This could be considered a good choice as an example ground for League One and Two in the EFL. Edgeley Park has a capacity of 10,841 (all seated). I will be watching the results of the Abbey Stadium trial with interest.

County's average in 2019/20 was 4,342 compared to a Cambridge average of 4,366 in League Two. Our average would put us in to the top 10 of League Two even though we currently ply our trade in the division below. In League Two (when we get there) we should be averaging over 5,000 and possibly over 6,000 if we are doing well making County one of the best supported teams in that division.

In conclusion to the attendance talk, we should be back in Edgeley Park by October watching the Hatters assault on the National League. Some fans forums have talked about the crowds being restricted at 25-30% of the stadium capacities. At County this would mean a maximum crowd of 2,710-3,252. This would be a shame seeing as we average 4,342. However, with the government wanting to get everything moving as quickly as possible related to the economy, bigger allowances are expected. If we could have a maximum 50% capacity that would be 5,420 which would be enough. One solution could be to re-open the Railway End to spread fans out a bit more.

19th July 2020

It is National League play-off day and I am watching Boreham Wood v Halifax in the play-off qualifying round. Live on TV from Boreham Wood's, neat and tidy re-developed ground called Meadow Park. A 5,000-capacity stadium including the North Bank behind one of the goals. They do have a Gunners connection with the Arsenal ladies playing home games there.

The result was 2-1 to the Wood. Shame for the Shaymen but I am happy as it means Halifax remain in the National

League next season providing a short distance away match. Boreham Wood play Harrogate in the play-off semi.

Yesterday Barnet beat Yeovil 2-0 away, so it looks like the team that usurped us to a play-off place on the points per game calculation may be progressing. Meanwhile in the National North play-offs Altrincham beat Chester 3-2. In the other National North play-off match Brackley play Gateshead. Not too bothered about that one as both are about the same distance travel-wise with Brackley somewhere near Milton Keynes and Gateshead being neighbours of Newcastle-upon Tyne of course.

Gateshead beat Brackley away 6-5 on pens after a 0-0 draw at the end of normal time.

The draw for the semis is York v Altrincham and Boston v Gateshead. In National League South it is Havant & Waterlooville v Dartford and Weymouth v Dorking. Kings Lynn are already promoted form the North and Wealdstone are already promoted form the South.

21st July 2020

Massive statement of intent yesterday. County signed John Rooney from National League champions Barrow for an un-disclosed fee. The 29-year-old scored 17 league goals last season, leading Barrow back into the EFL - and won two Player of the Year awards. Rumour is the fee is £75,000. Message boards and twitter have a few frustrated comments from Bluebirds fans wondering why John has not stayed with them as they are promoted to the Football League. There are two main factors. Firstly, from John's financial point of view is the three-year contract. Not many three-year contracts are handed out at this level.

More importantly for us and him is ambition. Barrow have just been promoted to the league above but County are clearly a much bigger club. We have double their home fans, a real football league ground, great established manager and new owner.

Plus, another signing! This time striker Alex Reid, 24, joins from Stevenage. A product of the Aston Villa youth system Reid has been on loan at several National League outfits providing good experience at this level. County manager Jim Gannon has been a fan for several years so let's trust in Jim.

We are on the start of a journey that should see us climb back to League One which is our natural level. New owner Mark Stott even has ambitions of a return to the Championship. Welcome aboard John and Alex. I have not been this excited about a new season for over twenty years. Go, Go County!

25th July 2020

Today is playoff semi-final day. The losers will play County again next season.

There is an update on the start date for the new season in the EFL. The Championship, League One and League Two will all start on Saturday 12th September. As it stands fans will only be allowed into the grounds from October. The first few games will be behind closed doors. There will also be updates as the weeks progress between now and then on the percentage capacity allowance. The other key question is, will away fans be allowed in?

The National League traditionally starts a week before the EFL which would mean a Saturday 5th September opening match for County. Fingers crossed for this date with supporters in the ground. Let's see how events pan out as August progresses. I am hoping for a positive development on fan attendance. Or somehow, I may have to gain a press pass or find other ways to watch County live from the start of the season.

Back to the semi-finals-

I will fill the results in below but I need to overview the action. Today was an entertaining day of football. Still behind closed doors but full of promotion pressure and passion. High scoring and full of drama. Football fans in general in this modern era would benefit by taking notice of "non-league" action. There are a growing number of disenfranchised supporters of big teams, especially Premier League clubs. Factors include cost to enter the ground, the difficulty of casual attendance, lack of opportunity for youths to go with their mates and ever-changing kick off times.

You cannot really blame the players for taking a slice of the mega commercial opportunities in the TV driven modern elite leagues. However, there is no doubt that even young fans dislike the prima donna antics and mercenary manipulation of contracts. Agents are partly to blame moving players on for profit before loyalty or even glory.

Lower leagues are refreshing once given a chance. Easy and affordable entry to matches. The ability for kids to attend with a group of mates. Less play-acting, diving or "simulation". Teams that have a core of British players. I am not xenophobic. Most fans would admit that victory feels more complete with some local players or players from their own country. Some Premier league matches struggle to field more than ten percent British players in the starting line-ups. In the lower leagues a significant amount of the players are local.

The pandemic may affect the financial set up of the big clubs and how much they pay their players. It may be a blessing in disguise and hopefully will result in the regulation of agents.

Back to the play-offs-...

National League - already promoted to League Two- Barrow (PS – thanks for John Rooney).

Semi's – Harrogate 1 v Boreham Wood 0 (so we play Boreham Wood next season)

Notts County 2 v Barnet 0 (we keep Barnet, the team that usurped us on points per game for a play-off spot)

It is down to Harrogate and Notts County for promotion to League Two in the play-off final. Who would I like to keep?

Notts County would be a great "big match" between two of the best supported teams in the league. However, they will be a real challenge to our promotion hopes. So I'd choose to keep Harrogate.

National League North

Already promoted to the National League- King Lynn Town

Semi-finals:

York 0 v Altrincham 2

Well done Alty who I have a soft spot for. My Granddad was from Altrincham so I've been to a few Alty games. A proper non-league giant over the years. This was their fourth win in a row away at York too. Shame for York though as they are about to move into a new stadium.

Boston United 5 v Gateshead 3

What a play-off battle this was. Boston also move into a new stadium soon so this will come as a bonus for them. With this one, the outcome in the Final I want is a no-brainer. It is Altrincham all the way simply as it provides a local derby only 6 miles away.

National League South

Already promoted to the National League- Wealdstone

Semi-finals:

Havant & Waterlooville 1 v Dartford 2

Weymouth 3 v Dorking Wanderers 2

To be perfectly honest, I don't have a preference for which team is promoted into our league. Weymouth is somewhere past Yeovil and on a level with Bournemouth so miles away for travel.

Dartford is probably a bit closer but stuck somewhere under the Dartford crossing, east of London which is a pain to get to. Purely from a selfish view I am basing this on which one is less of a pain in the arse to get to. I'll go for Weymouth as it must be a more scenic journey.

29th July 2020

As I mentioned earlier in the book, I am a glass half full kind of guy. We had some news yesterday and now I feel as if I may have been slightly too optimistic. I started this journal based on my excitement for the new season. New owners, a bit of cash to spend on new players and the club turning full time for the new campaign. As you will recall I had a full plan for away matches and even a scoring system to rate the experience. Unfortunately, reality has hit home. The pandemic may require me to amend my plans significantly.

Yesterday the National League announced a start date for the new season of the 3rd October. This has come as a bit of a shock. The Premier League and EFL start back on the 12th September and traditionally we would start a week earlier in the National League. It looks like the National League have decided that our season cannot start without fans in the stadium as it is essential that the clubs have this stream of revenue to survive. This means the season will run through until the end of May 2021.

The clubs have until the 15th August to announce their crowd management and Covid match day management strategy. This needs to be made public on their websites. Then it is presumed that season tickets will be sold. The other key factor is an announcement on what percentage of the capacity will be allowed to be used. This will vary depending on the stadium layout. The key being social distancing and entry/ exit plans for the movement of fans. No food and drink is expected to be sold. This may change as it is a key stream of revenue for clubs at our level.

Website streaming of matches should take place and subscriptions will provide another income source for the clubs. The most worrying aspect for my plans is that there is a possibility that there will be no away fans. This will scupper my ambitions of attending most or even all the matches this season. However, this will be part of the story in these weird and testing times. I will be at all the home games (hopefully) and will stream all the away matches if necessary.

In terms of home attendance my season ticket (plus my youngest sons ticket) will guaranty our place at the home league and cup matches. Some clubs have already started to sell season tickets but I presume they are limiting the numbers as they will not know their reduced capacity figure.

The Premier League and EFL start on the 12th September but at present no fans will be allowed in until October. Behind closed doors football will continue into the new season for them. Our crowd maybe reduced slightly but I predict we should still have somewhere near 4,000 fans in the ground as a maximum capacity. Below our 4,300 average in the 19/20 season. We would get nearer to 5,000 with the new players and optimism but that is unlikely to be allowed.

The weird result of reduced capacities will be more visible in the Premier League and Championship. This is likely to require every other row of seats being empty. Then social distancing between each season ticket holder or group of season ticket holders. For example, if Liverpool have a maximum thirty percent capacity that would be 16,000 and Man Utd would be 22,000. At Edgeley Park we would re-open the Railway End and then spread home fans across all four stands.

Every other row empty then a gap either side of me and Jonnie. So that would be two or three seats empty either side of us. I predict that attendances will be somewhere between thirty and forty percent of capacity.

Crowd management of circa 4,000 fans at Edgeley Park should be manageable. There is likely to be a reduction in chanting and atmosphere as the singers will be spaced apart. At the Premier League clubs 15,000 or 20,000 is going to be a challenge. Man Utd are likely to be playing in front of 20-25,000 at home. Strange times indeed. Hopefully Covid infection figures reduce rapidly and we can get back to normal asap.

1st August 2020

Today is play-off Final day in the National League North and South. Boston v Altrincham and Weymouth v Dartford. It is also the first day of the Scottish season which seems like a non-stop cavalcade of football. County will have to wait until the 3rd of October. Bad news over the last twenty-four hours is a partial lockdown in the Northwest due to increased Covid infections. Nationally, the opening of certain indoor businesses has been delayed. This includes cinemas etc. More worrying is the planned fan trials in stadiums have been postponed. Nevertheless, we should still be on for a 3rd October start.

Good news is that Jamie Stott has signed for the Hatters on a two-year deal. The former Oldham central defender has had a couple of loan spells with County already and was young player of the year in our 2018/19 Championship winning season.

Tomorrow is the Final for the National League promotion to League Two. The loser of Harrogate v Notts County will stay in the National League and play County again.

Results:

Boston 0 v Altrincham 1

Well done Alty and I am well chuffed with this result. Mainly because it provides a local derby for the new season but also as Altrincham have by all accounts been excellent this season and especially in the play-offs. I listened to the second half on Radio Robins. Initially just to keep up with the score but I stuck with it as Alty played the game out professionally. It was great to listen to how delighted the commentators were. Altrincham on their budget have done brilliantly and they have gone up and will remain semi-pro. Unfortunate for Boston as this was their last ever match at York Street before they move into their new stadium.

Weymouth 0 v Dartford 0

Weymouth win 3-0 on pens, so a more scenic away day journey albeit a longer trip in comparison to Dartford. I may be visiting the home of the Terras as they are known. To the Bob Lucas stadium. Not sure who Bob is/ was but the stadium is a decent size. It may all be in vain as it is unlikely that away fans will be allowed in to matches next season. Certainly not in the first few months anyway. 3-0 on pens. Dartford had a nightmare there!

2nd August 2020

It is play-off Final Day in the National League and I am watching the match live on BT Sports from Wembley stadium. I have been looking forward to tuning in to this match. Under normal circumstances I probably wouldn't have watched this. Normally, this match would have been done and dusted in May. The season would have finished as planned and I would have looked forward to a couple of months away from footy ready to go again in August.

After having no County related football since March, anything County connected is worth watching. The losers stay with us in the National League while the winners go up. Even though having Notts County in our league is a good thing, I want Harrogate to lose as they present a bit less of a threat to us next season.

Looking at Wembley on the TV screen brought back great memories of 2008 when we beat Rochdale 3-2 in the League Two play-off final. A great match and day out. Our 90's Wembley appearances were at the old Wembley and all ended in defeat. That Rochdale match was a game where I thought we were going to win it from the start of the match. We were on a great run of form in the second half of that season and a better side than Rochdale all around the pitch.

That was a great day in 2008 and we finally won at Wembley after all that 90's heartache. Four times we lost at Wembley in the early 90's. In hindsight though, the legacy of the 90's losses transpired into a much more satisfying conclusion. Despite those losses we were on a consistent upward trajectory for ten years from 1990. After 2008 due to financial problems the team was soon split up and we went on a downward spiral for ten years. Let us savour this new dawn.

The result is:

Harrogate Town 3 v Notts County 1

Harrogate were brilliant. This was an enjoyable match to watch. Notts County have far more experienced players but Harrogate had the energy and took their chances. Which made me think that we must get automatic promotion this coming season. The play-offs would be good but anything can happen in one off matches. Today proved this. Notts were favourites beforehand but were second best. Harrogate supporters will be pinching themselves. Could they have even dreamed of being a football league club only a few years ago? It just shows how football has changed when Salford and Harrogate are in the football league while Notts and Stockport County will play each other in the National League next year.

Arsenal v Chelsea in the FA Cup Final yesterday was a good watch too. Just need to get back to live football asap.

It is all confirmed now. I cannot wait for the 3rd October when the season starts.

This is the National League for 2020/2021-

1. Aldershot
2. Altrincham
3. Barnet
4. Boreham Wood
5. Bromley
6. Chesterfield
7. Dagenham & Redbridge
8. Dover Athletic
9. Eastleigh
10. FC Halifax Town
11. Hartlepool Utd
12. Kings Lynn Town
13. Maidenhead
14. Notts County
15. Solihull Moors

16. Stevenage or Macclesfield
17. Stockport County
18. Sutton Utd
19. Torquay Utd
20. Wealdstone
21. Weymouth
22. Woking
23. Wrexham
24. Yeovil

So there we go. Still southern biased in terms of numbers but at least Altrincham went up for a local derby and Halifax stayed down. Those two along with Wrexham and Chesterfield represent decent travelling distances. Solihull Moors, Notts County and Hartlepool are the next best. Then it is down the deep south (or the far east to Kings Lynn) for County away followers. Subject to restrictions on away fans being lifted.

This league has four teams beginning with W and one with Y. Which is a bit unusual.

Here is the map- You have got to feel sorry for Hartlepool!

4th August 2020

Tonight I am going to watch Brentford v Fulham in The Championship play off final. This match is claimed to be the most lucrative match in world football. Something like £160 million is at stake for the winners. This figure is the value of the TV deal Premiership teams receive plus the benefit of a parachute payment if you are relegated back to the Championship. The parachute lasts for two or three years which guarantees that you will have a financial advantage. Should be a good match too.

The result was 2-1 to Fulham after extra time. Cagey match with Fulham the better team throughout . Fulham left back Bryan got both their goals.

You may be thinking whether this has any connection to County. Well we did finish eighth once and just outside the play-off spots for entry into the Premier League. Also, it could be argued that we are or have been at the same level as Brentford for a good part of our history. The size of the club is roughly the same with a similar catchment area for supporters. It just highlights what is possible. Bournemouth, who have just been relegated from the Premier League fall into the same category. Anything is possible and we can now dream of an ascent up the football league.

Man Utd are reported to be almost there in the negotiations to sign Jadon Sancho from Borussia Dortmund. I have been banging on about John Rooney to my two sons in the last few weeks. They have smiled at me each time with what I think is football respect. A middle-aged County fan excitedly talking about one of Wayne Rooney's brothers who has just signed for a non-league club.

I even think they are getting a bit excited about the new season for the Hatters. Jonnie has started wearing his County shirt from a few seasons ago. It is a pleasure to have football banter with my sons. We can talk enthusiastically about not only a Champions League team but also the mighty Stockport County.

11th August 2020

It has been announced by the EFL that Macc are relegated into our league. Stevenage have been upgraded to 23rd in League 2. Macc have been docked four more points due to their financial transgressions. The points per game formula predicted that Macc would have accrued less points now the four have been taken off.

It is a relief to have another local derby. In our southern biased league it is great to have another Cheshire team. I feel sorry for their fans. However, us football fanatics have little sympathy for the opposition when we play them. I had a soft spot for Macc which was slightly tainted when they stuffed us 6-0 at the Moss Rose in 2005. A real low point for me stood behind the goal that day. It looks like Macc are following in our footsteps down the leagues as we are ascending. Good luck to Macc apart from our two matches next season when I look forward to six points as we progress.

CHAPTER SIX
Pre-Season Preparation

With the play-offs concluded and the Hatters opponents confirmed for next season, it is time for final prep for the new campaign. Time to consult the fixture list and log the away match locations and dates. There are a higher-than-average long distance away days this season.

NB- attendance of away matches is still not confirmed but If I can, I will attend away matches. As with any book written under such strange circumstances it is hard to predict when away matches can be partaken . Or when away fans will be allowed in.

The long-distance traveller is something that is not unusual for me. In perfect preparation for the long distance away days forthcoming in 20/21 I have decided to recall some of my travels in pursuit of hobbies or interests. Perfect prep for Dover or Torquay away. When I started this log, my natural enthusiasm was evident. As I write over the weeks, the sensible switch comes on and you reflect on whether it is a good idea. In my career, in my younger days I remember one large Yorkshire company director refer to me as the impulsive one. If you look up the word impulsive, I reckon that 80% of the definitions are positive. I would say that I was enthusiastic. Once I get the buzz for an idea the enthusiasm usually carries me through.

In addition to my football fandom, I am also I big fan of music in general. Especially rock music. Rock music has a similar effect as football on its supporters. Both have a sense of loyalty and uniform. Fans will go to some lengths to follow the team or band. Before emigrating to the States in January 82 (for four years), I had started a dual interest between rock music and football.

The music side was cemented with a visit to Manchester Apollo in late 1981 to see Gillan in concert. This is the fellow that was the singer in Deep Purple before pursuing a successful solo career. As a 14-year-old, I became slightly obsessed with following these pass-times. Moving to the States allowed me to see a golden era of rock around LA. In recent years I've produced a memoir of these days in book form. I've also been a rock reviewer for various magazines and followed bands across Europe.

NB- at this point some people may be thinking- "get on with it mate, this a County book"- so I'll get to the point.

OK, so football fans and music fans do a fair few away days. The analogy is my travels via motorcycle (and other forms of transport) into Germany, Belgium and France to see rock bands. On one occasion, the return trip from a festival in Dortmund (all the way back to Cheshire) was made with failing rear wheel bearings. This created a lateral juddering sensation for nigh on 600 miles. So, I will not complain about Torquay away.

On another occasion, and another rock festival, I travelled back from Nantes (mid-France) with a fuel saving condition called valve failure. This is where an engine wants to cut out at every traffic light. Fortunately, I managed to get back to Cheshire without hardly stopping. Unfortunately, this resulted in a serious motorcycling condition called PNA (nothing to do with PNE- Preston North End).

This is a condition known amongst bikers as Permanent Numb Arse. You may be relieved to know (I certainly will be), that for Hatters away days next season I will utilise a modern automobile. Pretty much bulletproof with power steering, electric windows, air conditioning and all the mod cons. I still have a motorbike and had a fleeting idea of attending all County away days next season on my trusty Royal Enfield with a County flag blowing in the wind. But I'm too old for all that crap.

NB- I have had a re-think and I may attend a fair few games on the Royal Enfield and combine some football trips with motorbiking. Might make it a bit more interesting!

Here we are at the dawn of the new season. How many matches will I attend? I do not know at this stage. I am up for it as they say. The more I think about it, the more I think of those travelogues of these crazy dudes that travel around the world on a moped or a bicycle. I have a mate who went from Exeter Uni in 1985 on an old 250cc motorbike all the way to Cape Town. No sat nav, no fuel gauge (bikes just had a reserve tank tap that you turned on if the engine spluttered) and no mobile phone. The engine blew up somewhere in east Africa, several punctures followed and he camped out. Now that takes balls. So, come on Taylor, stop whinging and get on with the job.

Family negotiation

The job in hand pre-season, entails forward planning fixture clash avoidance preparation. The wife is now in complete awareness of the extent of this plan. Kath did not display an over enthusiastic reaction to my declaration of the distances involved. At first there was a "that means every weekend will be devoted to football" statement. At which point I explained that at least there are some solid times to the matches unlike the Premier league. I proclaimed that it would be a lot more onerous as a Premier League fan as the kick-off times could be at any time on any day of the week. Also, those times and days are subject to change at the whim of the TV companies.

As County do not have the current standing to be involved in TV deals, we are guaranteed our kick-off times. 3pm Saturday home or away. Or 7:45pm on a Tuesday. I was looking for a flicker of comfort or enthusiasm in Kath's eyes and demeanour but the flicker was very slight and I proceeded to continue with my reasoning. I confirmed that I would indeed be free every Sunday for my youngest son's football matches.

I said the above shortly after confirmation of a week away in the Cairngorms, Scotland. I had strategically preferred a week in early August to avoid the slight chance that the new season might have started at the end of August. I felt slightly devious preferring early August but when challenged with a football fixture list these are the tactics that are required. I am glad this is likely to be a one season exercise. I sometimes wonder how some fans get away with attending matches while keeping wives happy. Or maybe they don't, as they no longer have one (a wife that is).

For the sake of my marriage and this book to a lesser extent, I missed out on a car touring trip. My Mum re-married after my Dad passed away. The chap, Tony, is a rather entertaining gentleman. He is also a petrol-head. That doesn't mean he is addicted to sniffing petrol (well, not as far as I know). This means he really likes cars and refurbishes old "classics". These have included an ancient Citroen, a "Bergerac" Jag, a 90's Aston Martin and now a "classic" Saab. My mother simply refuses to get in the Saab. After a few classic car trips, she now refuses to attend road trips or car shows. Tony is fanatical about these events and has tried to recruit me on occasion. A trip to the world Saab convention in Sweden was planned in August but postponed due to coronavirus. This was to be completed in the Saab which would have been a decent adventure.

Tony's natural enthusiasm uncovered another option and a driving tour in Spain was offered to me as co-driver/ navigator/ fellow bon viveur. This was to take place in late September which I had to declare was a clash with potential County fixtures. Not to be perturbed, and as a good salesman, Tony countered with another option. Why don't I spice the book up by comparing County with lower league Spanish teams that may be en route? Siguenza and Santander were suggested as potential match locations. I could then report back to a mate who went to the County games and compare notes. Not a bad idea and if I were a single man, it could have been an option. However, after recent careful negotiations with the missus and strategic planning to accommodate potential football fixtures, I politely declined.

Again, Tony came back with another idea. How about he joins me on some of these County away days. He has friends near Yeovil, Torquay, Dover and Bromley. This idea could spread the cost of fuel etc and provide somewhere to stop over. Good idea and it covers some of the long-distance fixtures. I am not sure if he would attend the matches. He is a City fan born in Wythenshawe but lived most of his life in Stockport. Therefore, in my opinion, as a time served Stopfordian, he is duty bound to attend the games or be shamed.

In terms of County recruitment, I have spent a fair slice of my time trying to convince people into the charms of County. Usually this falls on deaf ears. Unless County are in the throes of a successful run with media attention. For example, in the Danny Bergara years the Hatters got regular local TV coverage. With Wembley play-off and Cup appearances the casual fans started coming back and it was easier to recruit the odd "newbie."

In the Dave Jones/ Andy Kilner era and the heady days of playing Man City (and usually beating them), suddenly more mates would attend. But once normal service resumed and County struggled to win games the casuals fell away and the hardcore loyalists remained. The same faces etched with wry smiles from gallows humour. Some you had seen for years without talking to them. Nods of recognition would be exchanged at Edgeley Park and far-flung lower league outposts.

Here we are at the dawn of a new era. Positivity prevails. County are on the way back. It has been a long haul with a few years in the sixth tier of English football. Many fans under the age of thirty won't remember the heady days of the 1990's. A new generation of County fans celebrated the National League North championship as the most successful event in their County supporting life. Now, with a decent head of steam the Hatters will progress back up the leagues in a new golden period.

The team have been back in training for about a month. The sessions are taking place at Edgeley Park. This is part of the back to work programme whereby you need to return to your main workplace. Soon County will take residence at their new training ground at Carrington. I know Carrington well as my youngest son Jonnie trained there when he was in the Bury FC academy.

The training centre County will share is the Sale FC Rugby training facility at Carrington. This initially rang alarm bells among County fans with memories of the Sale Sharks debacle and the Brian Kennedy era. This was when the egg chasers took over Edgeley Park and depleted the football side of the business. To be clear Sale FC are the original amateur rugby club. Nothing to do with Sale Sharks, so a bit of relief once that was confirmed. The training ground is excellent and the Stockport County training centre signs are up. Happy days.

I have been re-united with my Royal Enfield Himalayan motorbike a potential form of County watching transport. Earlier in the summer I had some engine problems which were exacerbated when I broke down on the Grane Road between Haslingden and Blackburn. I was visiting a mate in Accrington. The engine issue had been going on for a while but with lockdown in place all the bike shops were shut.

So I persisted with the problem until the bike finally packed up on the scenic Grane Road. It had an idle problem which meant I had to keep the revs up at traffic lights or when stationary. On this occasion it lost all compression in the engine. It struggled to start. After repeated attempts and tinkering I stopped. The battery was almost dead. At this point I deduced that I made three errors-

1. I did not have breakdown cover on my insurance policy- I felt like a bit of a tight arse at this point.

2. I was stranded thirty-five miles from home in lockdown- I was flouting non-essential travel rules and could be arrested / reprimanded by the strong arm of the law.
3. I was bloody minded and persisted with a bike that had no tick-over or idle.

The saving grace was I was aiming downhill back towards home. If I lived up hill towards Blackburn, I would have been stuffed! I put the bike in neutral and rolled downhill gaining speed. Checking the speedo I got up to 40 mph which is some speed without a working engine. I knew I could get to Haslingden using this technique. Then it was just the other thirty bloody miles to consider. While coasting at high speed I decided on a shit or bust option. A potentially dangerous engine starting technique. I gave a press on the starter switch. Like a miracle the engine just fired up. I pulled the clutch lever and kicked up to fourth gear. Anything less and I would have jolted and gone base over apex.

I did not stop otherwise the bike would have died. I went along the M60 off the exit ramp at Stockport West, around the pyramid roundabout and up Didsbury Road. Without stopping for traffic lights, man or beast. I got to about a mile from home and the engine just gave up. Then I pushed my iron horse home.

A lucky escape and the bike is finally back from the garage with a new engine head all paid for under warranty. Happy days. The moral to this tale is get roadside recovery in your insurance policy and don't be a tight arse.

You may be asking yourself that was a bit non-County? Aah well, I have decided that I really missed the olde girl and the Royal Enfield will feature as a mode of County watching transport this coming season. I have even procured some rather brilliant County stickers to stick to the front screen of the bike. Result.

And finally, for the pre-season prep chapter. Today, the 10th August 2020, an announcement was made about the best signing of them all. Mr Jim Gannon our inimitable manager has signed a full-time contract until June 2022. This season will see Jim's 1000th game for County as player and manager. A living legend and along with Danny Bergara, the most important individuals in the history of the Hatters.

I said earlier in the book that Danny was the most important. Danny took us from perennial losers to consistent winners. However, Jim was part of that as a player and a saviour as a manager. Several years in the sixth tier of English football could have written us off. Jim has kept County alive and now there is light at the end of the tunnel. I have changed my mind. Danny and Jim are joint legends.

Today was the first day at the new Carrington training facility. It is rated as a Championship level centre. We are on the up. I might just take a ride out on the Royal Enfield and have a look tonight. It is the little things in life that keep me happy. Or as the rest of the family say. "You are just bonkers".

CHAPTER SEVEN
Stockport

OK, with the summer diary complete and pre-season preparations discussed it is time to get to the crux of the matter: The National League season 2020/21. One that is looking very promising for County with the new squad assembled and ready to go. We are favourites and it is all to play for. No pressure lads! But before we get down to business and I take you through how it all panned out, I wanted to pay homage to the town of Stockport.

I am setting the scene for the place that Stockport County represents. Unlike American sports where teams are franchises and at the mercy of being uprooted, English football is sacrosanct. We wouldn't allow a situation such as the Oakland Raiders becoming the LA Raiders, then back to Oakland before becoming the Las Vegas Raiders. English football clubs are inextricably linked with their towns. They gain nicknames from the industry of their towns. County and Luton are both called the Hatters and Scunthorpe are nicknamed The Iron for example.

Of course, there are times when English football owners and chairmen attempt sacrilege. We of course had our very own Brendan Ellwood suggesting re-locating to Maine Rd and becoming Man Stock County! Famously, Oxford owner Robert Maxwell proposed a merger between Oxford and Reading creating a hybrid club called the Thames Valley Royals. Apart from the fact the name sounds like a baseball team the whole idea was ridiculed. In both cases Maxwell and Ellwood were laughed at and had to scrap their un-workable ideas. Both left their clubs shortly after blushing with embarrassment.

I was going to give this chapter a title like "It's got a lot to answer for" or "Up the North". I have put a fair bit of effort into this book but I'm not going to spend much time trying to come up with a cool title for a chapter just for the sake of it. This chapter is called Stockport because I like it. This is my hometown. Just like folk are from Mansfield, Ashton in Makerfield or Monaco. Each has its charm, hidden secrets and architectural history. Seasoned travellers recommend that you look up in a town or city. Walk down the street but look up and see the architecture. Then you notice the roof lines, parapets, finials, window heads and detail of the facades. Look at the pavement and a lateral perspective and you miss so much. There is plenty to admire in Stockport.

Most know the charms of Chester, York, Cambridge, Oxford, Edinburgh, London and even Manchester. It is recorded in the memory of school trips, tourist guides and advertising. Stocky as I like to affectionately refer to, is as good as Chester in my eyes. Our town has a similar potential. Are you mad mate, I hear you decry?

I will admit the River Dee in Chester has much more impact than the trickle of the Mersey under Mersey Square. However, go up to the impeccably restored market hall and walk to Underbank and Hillgate and you will find a warren of bridges, stairways and shabby chic shops and pubs such as the Cracked Actor. When I say shabby chic, I don't mean anything with an air of pretention. The "olde" streets of Underbank and Hillgate contain genuine old buildings. Many untouched since the 1960's.

Partly due to under investment these buildings have been underused for decades. Being so close to Manchester has not helped from an investment potential. Slowly some of these old wrecks are coming to life. Like Chester's famous rows (shopping arcades) the shops of olde town Stockport have tremendous potential. Stockport's topography lends itself to character. I just hope they do not gentrify it too much.

OK, there you go, my Stockport Council tour guide application has been submitted. But I can assure you, I am completely sold on the charms of good olde Stocky.

Stockport is also home to a major brewery in the town centre. Robinsons (Robbies) is a fantastic original building and home to the legendary Old Tom strong beer. This has developed itself into a chocolate Tom and other specialist ales as Robbies have diversified in to one of the most successful breweries in the country. Robbie's is home of Trooper beer the signature ale of the rock band Iron Maiden. Apparently, due to the global popularity of the band, the Trooper collection, at one point, had the highest on-line beer sales in the world. There is a great museum in the brewery that has an Iron Maiden Trooper section. Of course, as a rock fan, I have paid a visit and met Maidens lead singer Bruce Dickinson when he did a book signing there for his autobiography.

Importantly, Robbie's was the shirt sponsor for County in the 90's when The Hatters made their ascent up the football league. It would be good to get them back on the shirts.

This could be a good moment for a potted history of my connection to grand olde Stocky. I was born in a terraced house in Offerton with an outside toilet. For some reason, I came into the world in the front bedroom of the two up two down. My grandparents had the off license two doors down on the corner just off Hall Street. They then had a sweet shop on Brinny (Brinnington) estate.

My Granddad became caretaker at Offerton High School and lived in the house next to the school gates. Somehow my parents moved to a four-bed detached house on a posh 70's estate in Torkington, Hazel Grove. Until the money ran out and we had to move to Bolton. A family friend had got a good deal on a new house in Lancs. We then moved to LA before a move back to Offerton. You could say that was a long way back round to Edgeley Park. LA to Edgeley!

So, here we are in August 2020 at the dawn of a new season with one of the best squads we could have assembled. County fans have a team that will do the town proud. Let us see Stockport back on the map and the team back in the Football League. Read how it pans out in the following chapters. A month-by-month review of the fixtures in League and Cups.

CHAPTER EIGHT
August 2020

Hold your horses. Just when you thought it was safe to start the big kick-off, all sorts of last- minute amendments and curveballs are pitched my way. Writing a chronicle under these pandemic conditions is a nightmare. In terms of continuity that is. It is great though. It has provided plenty of content you wouldn't normally get in a typical pre-season. Normally pre-seasons are a bit boring.

Usually I want a break from footy then after a couple of weeks I am itching to get back. Then nothing happens. You get the kit launch. The odd signing and mundane preseason friendlies.

In 2020, it has all gone crazy. Macc have just been demoted into our league. On the 11th August! Normally we are two games into the new season by now. I have had enough of the summer diary. Let's get it on. We know we are starting on the 12th September and the latest from the National League is that we get our fixture list on the 8th September.

We have a first pre-season match too. This Saturday the 15th August we have the first match v Fleetwood. Live, free stream on the County website. Behind closed doors. I will be in Scotland on "staycation". Somewhere near Pitlochrie. We are staying in a cottage in a town called Blairgowrie. Looks good but I need to pack some midge repellent.

In my temporary Scottish home I will be pre-recording my Classic Album Tracks Show for GMRR (Greater Manchester Rock Radio) and tuning into the County website stream. I am sure Kath will be delighted. We have been married for over 20 years, so I must be doing something right. I think.

15th August - County 0 v 2 Fleetwood pre-season friendly at Carrington

The pre-season friendly is one for the connoisseur. The hardcore fan who has missed footy so much during the summer that they are just desperate to see the lads in action again. Often our first pre-season match is Cheadle Town or Cheadle Heath Nomads which falls into the hardcore category.

I have been to a few pre-season games over the years but I usually save myself for the real thing. The first match of the official season. There are exceptions such as when we may have signed someone high profile which rarely happens. I suppose you could call John Rooney high profile at out level.

In '95 we played a pre-season friendly against City when the new Cheadle End opened in front of a full house of nearly 11,000. I think that may still be a record attendance for the newly configured Edgeley Park. The figure was boosted by having no segregation areas that day and the ground was full. The record attendance for Edgeley Park through-out history is 27,833 v Liverpool in 1950 for the 5th round of the FA Cup. That was when the Pop side was twice the size before it was reduced in the 1970's.

Today, I did watch the first pre-season friendly. Kick off was 1:30pm and the match was played at our new Carrington training ground. They moved it from EP. The match was shown from 3:30pm on the County channel. I watched in the evening on return from our drive out to Glenshee as we are in Scotland on holiday. I thought it best to wait. Kath wouldn't have appreciated a curtailed visit of the beautiful Cairngorm national park. Not for a pre-recorded pre-season work out from our new training ground.

We lost 2-0 to Fleetwood. 2-0 at half time, clean sheet in the second half against a team that lost in the play-offs to get into the Championship. So decent. Jim Gannon made several changes for the second half and it was a good first runout for the new squad. Jon Keighren our club commentator did a

BACK NEXT YEAR! The Story of Following Stockport County & the 20/21 season

great job and I thanked him on twitter. John is great. Super-enthusiastic and his love for County shines through. The camera angle was a bit flat as I presume our club camera man was stood on a box.

We have signed winger Jordan Williams from Fylde. The 27-year-old gets a two-year contract. Full time that is. Just to remind myself that we are now full time professional. With players on two or even three-year contracts providing stability that we've not had for years. Jordan has played thirty games for Rochdale in the past providing solid football league experience. Last season the winger scored fifteen goals in thirty-seven appearances for Fylde. That is a good scoring return for a winger. Sounds like a good addition to the squad.

Stockport County offers me more satisfaction than topflight football. Some will understand. If you know, you know. Or if you are a bit bonkers. I think I am a bit of both! Anyhow, the enthusiasm for County and the new season is starting to rub off on the lads. Jonnie seems genuinely excited about the possibility of County winning the National League and a return to the Football League.

When you are 15 it is important that your team is winning. There were many times in the last ten years when it was a losing battle convincing the boys of the charms of County. Man Utd offers a lot more at their age. Now I have a chance of re-recruiting the lads. The National League North championship was the hors d'oeuvre. This new fully professional team is the main course. Do not let me down County!

22nd August - County 0 v 2 Rochdale pre-season friendly

The first Edgeley Park friendly ended up 2-0 to Rochdale. It is better to be playing League 1 sides and stretching the players rather than playing local non-league sides. The main difference in the first two matches has been an extra speed of thought in attack by the opposition. Physically we are a match but it is just that quicker thinking that League 1

-83-

players have. Whereby they take advantage of a defensive mistake. The more the lads play together, the more this telepathy will develop.

25th August - County 1 v 0 Salford City pre-season friendly

In the next pre-season friendly we beat League Two Salford 1-0 with a goal by new boy Alex Reid. Again played at EP behind closed doors County were the better team which bodes well.

NB- there you have it. Quite possibly the shortest chapter in football book history. August is traditionally the month of several league matches and the start of the league cup or whatever cup we are in at the time. Back in the olden times of my youth, County seemed to kick off each season with a home and away league cup tie. It tended to be Wigan if my memory serves me right. But here we are at the dawn of a new golden era for County and the blasted virus has decimated the August fixture list. A couple of behind closed doors pre-season friendlies providing the only action of note. Roll on September.

CHAPTER NINE
September 2020

Saturday 5th September 2020

Colne FC 0 v County 2 Pre-season friendly

Finally, a fixture County fans can attend. Northern Premier League side Colne are allowing 400 fans into their ground with a Covid regime in place. The tickets went on sale at 9am on Saturday 29th August on the Colne website. By 9:30am the County tickets had gone. Not sure what the split is but there will be Hatters fans in the Colne end. I managed to get one ticket. I tried to get one for Jonnie but the system wouldn't let me buy a child one. So I checked out and went back round to buy a second adult one but by then the tickets were sold out. The anticipation for the new season has led the County faithful to scramble for tickets for a pre-season friendly at Colne.

I have dedicated this match to the Royal Enfield as the mode of transport. I know East Lancs well having worked around there for a few years in the 90's. There is a scenic route which subject to weather I will plan out. I tend to avoid motorways and will probably go up through Rawtenstall over the tops to Burnley and then a back route over to Colne. Although Burnley can never be described as beautiful it is surrounded by some great countryside. There is the scenic Ribble Valley and the West Yorkshire route over towards Haworth. Even the barren moors towards Rossendale and over to Hebden Bridge have a certain charm. The only problem is the likelihood of precipitation up in the hills. On a sunny day that neck of the woods is great. Better check the weather app.

Before I get into the charms of Colne and the football-match I have a squad update. We have signed ex- Derby keeper Josh Barnes. We needed another goalie as back-up to Ben Hinchliffe. Right back Macauley Southam-Hales arrives from Fleetwood Town. Is that the full squad? We must be getting close to cover for all positions. Strength in depth.

The stadium is a bit like Accrington's ground in the respect that it allows views of hills in the background. The Colne ground is literally on the top of a hill looking down on Colne in the valley and the hills towards Yorkshire in the distance. The pitch is cut out of the hill and has the biggest slope I have ever seen.

Apparently, lockdown has delayed the construction of a new stadium financed by their wealthy Chairman. It is a nice little ground with a home end full of flags. On arrival I join a long queue for a bottle of water to re-hydrate and a pie for sustenance. Clearly not anticipating the invasion of about 300 County fans the concession hut struggles with demand. It takes the whole of the first half to get served.

There are steps to stand on so the view is OK and I am stood next to one of Richard Landon's (the County kitman) sons waiting to be served. He spends the half telling me about how he is the ball boy at the Railway end for home matches. I ask him if he has to retrieve the ball if it goes into the new houses behind the stand. He tells me that's his Dad's job. So I have an image of Richard Landon legging it down Hardcastle Road and jumping over the fence of the building site where the new houses are being built. I then have banter with a Burnley fan who annoyingly recalls their Wembley win over us. Also with a chap from Wigan whose son is in the Colne midfield and explains that half their team are players let go by Fleetwood.

In the second half County fans changed ends into the Colne end and a minor fight breaks out. Though I had friendly banter with a Burnley fan some younger elements couldn't be so magnanimous. The "aggro" lasted about ten seconds and at the end of the match there was a total over reaction by the Lancashire constabulary. Eight police vehicles lined the path back down to the housing estate near the ground.

Happy days and the joys of lower-league football. The match itself was a typical pre-season affair. Colne looked lively but County looked composed. John Rooney looked sharp. The team changed at half time. Nyal Bell apparently got some stick off a lone Stockport detractor but received enthusiastic chants from County fans at the end. Adam Thomas got both goals. One was technically an own goal as a Colne player got a touch. The other a looping header off a Jamie Stott cross.

All in all a decent game, good pre-season progress and the chance to see live football. Next up is Curzon Ashton at EP behind closed doors. Then on the 15th September County play a behind closed doors friendly versus Guiseley.

Nearly forgot the scores! My ad-hoc away day scoring system. Which may now be severely limited by the pandemic

Ground- 4 points (out of five)- picturesque, the sun was out over the rolling hills of Pendle. There was a neat little main stand and a roof behind one goal where the Colne ultras hung their rather impressive flags.

Fans- 4 points – there were about ten "chanters". They had a song something like "we are the reds, the pride of Lancs". Fair play. They had a Burnley fan in with them who antagonised our County "youth". A ten second handbags ensued before a convoy of police vehicles greeted the departing fans post-match. Good overtime if you can get it.

Pies- 4.5- I asked the concession hut man his choice of pies. His first was chicken and ham which sounded good. He then reeled off an impressive array of flavours. Mince & onion, cheese and onion, meat and potato, steak. I kept saying chicken and ham after each choice and he finally gave me my request. Bloody lovely too.

Beer/Drink- 1- On this occasion I didn't drink the beer. I'll put it down to the Southern Comfort and coke with lime and some other accoutrement that my mate mixed up the night before. That plus the beer. So the bottle of water was welcome hydration. So it gets a 1.

Early September activity included the season ticket renewals. Got mine and one for Jonnie. As predicted the crowd will be limited to 2,700. Roughly twenty five percent of capacity. The 1,900 season ticket holders renewed and 800 went on general sale and were snapped up by the eager Stockport public. Mine are in the middle of the Pop Side.

Not sure how the social distancing will pan out.

As predicted, County are utilising the Railway End to spread the 2,700 lucky souls around the ground.

Not sure how lucky they will feel when it's lashing it down in the middle of December. The Railway End is lacking a roof. Our new owners have hinted of a roof being added to protect the hardy occupants.

Hopefully by Xmas the crowd allowance will increase to 40%. Then, mercifully, the virus will subside and away fans will be back to boost the atmosphere.

Speaking of atmosphere and banter with away fans, the fixture list was released on the 8th September. This is a traditional highpoint of anticipation for supporters pre-season preparation. Especially, when you have a good squad assembled for the new campaign. Like us Hatters fans.

The typical fan looks for key dates such as our-
• First match- 3rd October – away to Torquay
• Boxing Day- Altrincham away (nice one)
• First home match- Halifax quickly followed by Dover
• Local derbies- Macc & Alty in December
• Big matches- Wrexham, Chesterfield & Notts County

Then we have all the southern teams including the Wealdstone Raider!

So all we can hope for is a return to normal. Get those away fans into EP and let the County hordes back on the road.

Saturday 12th September 2020

County 2 v Curzon Ashton 0 (behind closed doors friendly)

The Hatters play another pre-season friendly at home. This time we have neighbours "the Nash" from Ashton. A decent National League North side that have just taken our Alex Curran on loan who is a promising youngster. It just shows how our squad has developed when we can let Alex go out on loan. I have some good memories of the "Nash" and their Tameside Stadium. The ground is used for youth cup finals. My son Jonnie won a cup there a few years ago, his first experience of playing in a stadium. It is a nice ground with a large main stand and covered terrace on the opposite side.

The Tameside Stadium was opened in 2005 and features a statue of Geoff Hurst outside. A surprise to me, our World Cup 66 hero was born in the borough of Ashton. The statue is a competitor to the Old Trafford statue of Law, Best and Charlton. Geoff is joined by Jimmy Armfield (fellow 1966 World Cup winner) and Simone Perrotta who won the World Cup in 2016 with Italy. The connection being that all three were born in Ashton.

A couple of years ago I remember a great day out at Curzon on our way to lifting the National North title. What started as a few beers at the Tameside Stadium developed into a full session. County won and we made our way back to the bus station and decided to drop into what transpired to be probably the roughest bar in Ashton. It was entertaining though as there was a karaoke session already ongoing with an older lady banging out a version of the Led Zep song "Rock n Roll".

This was at 5:15pm. They only sold cans and a couple of draught beers. The bar is downstairs on the market if you would like to go. After one can we paid our thanks to the barman and left. Then we got a bus that meandered through Dukinfield and Hyde before we alighted at one of the real ale pubs in Stocky.

Again this establishment was full of characters and alcoholics. The rest of the afternoon/ evening included live bands at the Arden Arms and Spinning Top which had various well-known County fans in attendance. A County win, beer and bands. The perfect day.

To the actual match, this was another behind closed doors affair. The coverage is excellent on the County stream. Our media standard has stepped up since the takeover. It was always good with Jon Keighren an excellent commentator. The new media people are young guys that have lifted us to Premier league quality.

All the branding and on-screen graphics are perfect now. Watching on my tablet the quality is HD. It was good to see the new dugouts. There are large blue technical areas on Astroturf. The dugouts are bigger including new padded seats for the back-room staff and squad members.

When I renewed my season ticket last week, I noticed that the entrance to the Pop side area has been re-clad in County Blue. There are horizontal rails ready for brand new cladding panels for the whole of the back of the Cheadle End.

The existing cladding has faded in colour over the years since it was built in 95. Presumably, the new cladding with be the County blue with the new badge.

The Hatters beat Curzon 2-0. Rooney was man of the match. He is quality, composed and he rarely gives the ball away. Most of our moves and chances involved Rooney. Curzon were decent but we restricted them to one good chance which was a defensive mistake.

The defence, other than that one chance, looked solid. The only slight improvement could be our goals per possession rate. In the first half we should have been 3 or 4 up rather than 2-0.

When we play National League opposition, we need to put our chances away to be top of the league. All in all a promising and solid pre-season so far. Three wins in a row now and no goals conceded. Scorers were Reid and Thomas.

Alex Reid looks particularly good and his work rate will impress Jim Gannon. I can see Jim having Alex as one of the first on the team sheet.

Tuesday 15th September 2020

Guiseley 1 v County 5 (behind closed doors friendly)

Guiseley is located between Bradford and Leeds in West Yorkshire. I have been contemplating how I could attend some of these behind closed doors games. It is almost impossible at EP as it is a proper stadium and has security. There are some grounds that have a hill or higher ground to stand outside and see most of the pitch. When I thought of higher ground, I suddenly had Red Hot Chilli Peppers or Stevie Wonder playing in my cranium.

At Guiseley it is flat as a pancake around the ground. However, the walls bordering part of the stadium are probably eight foot tall. I could take my light aluminium step ladder, park up near the back of the ground and get a perfect view of the match. Or I could just watch it in HD on my tablet in the comfort of my own home. Using Google maps you can literally case out all the grounds. When or if my wife Kath reads this, she will realise that I am indeed a bit of a nutter. It is a bug that grips footy fans who go to crazy lengths to follow their teams.

For Guiseley, I am predicting a little less security compared to say Notts County or Chesterfield. For the "proper" league stadiums the perimeter is usually monitored and the stands too big to look over. At Nethermoor Park, I am thinking that the car park and main entrance will have security to keep fans out and sign in the players and officials. Opposite the main stand looks like a path and a wooded area near houses. Perfect for my step ladder. My head will be visible but I may go unnoticed.

This plan rules out the Royal Enfield. A step ladder strapped to the side of a motorbike traversing the M62 is not a good idea. Especially when you reach the summit near Oldham which is the highest point of any motorway in England. Plus, I assume it is illegal. The ladder would act as a sail and possibly dump me in that farm that splits the M62 somewhere near Huddersfield. So it will be the Audi. Dependable German transport and plenty of room for the step ladder.

Today's work schedule is a meeting in Liverpool, then in the office in St Helens, back home, drop Jonnie off at football training near the centre of Manchester then up to Guiseley. Step ladder on board. As I am over 25,000 words into the book I may as well stick to the theme and make the effort of seeing County in action. The original plan before lockdown was to attend as many County games as possible home and away. The pandemic has cramped my style somewhat. I was at Colne so I have attended the maximum available. Thus far I am one out of one. So Guiseley it is. The second possible match to attend.

I set out for West Yorkshire with the usual tingle of excitement when travelling to the match. The loyal fan will tell you that when their team is playing there is an emotional pull to be at the game. The experience is not quite the same watching on TV. In fact, non-attendance can really bug you especially if there was a possibility of being there. This season is a little different as fans will not be allowed into a lot of the away matches. There is only so much you can do. That includes somehow viewing the pitch without entry into the ground.

It is a balmy evening about 25 degrees C and unusually warm for September. The M62 rises over Saddleworth Moor near Oldham. The vivid green fields and clear blue skies are a pleasant contrast. Carlos Santana echoes chilled out tones as I cross the border into Yorkshire. Life is good. With plenty of time at hand I will stop off for some tea. Maybe fish and chips. Or maybe something healthy such as a quinoa salad. Do they sell quinoa in West Yorkshire? I contemplate what it might taste like and decide to stay safe and look for a chippy.

The micro-climate that is Saddleworth Moor turns the skies cloudy and stormy as soon as I descend towards West Yorkshire. The forecast says no rain but the clouds look decidedly moist and a few drops impact my windscreen. I come off the M62 and realise that Guiseley is one of those places that isn't near a motorway junction.

Usually the motorway network can drop you off within touching distance of most towns. This destination is kind of north of Bradford and Leeds. Not close to the M62 or M1/A1. So almost half the journey time is spent meandering fifteen miles through the Bradford suburbs. After a slight diversion due to a sat nav malfunction I park up at the cricket club next to the ground.

I suddenly had a touch of self-consciousness as I looked at my step ladder. I left it in the car as I walked the perimeter of the stadium. It was evident that I was the lone nutter contemplating an "illegal" view of the match. I peered in the cricket field club house and the TV was fixed on the stadium as the match was being shown. I thought about joining the couple watching the screen and having a pint. I then thought it was a bit daft to travel fifty miles to watch it on a telly in a building next to the ground.

I could hear the dulcet tones of Jim Gannon urging his players on as they prepared for kick off. I thought I better make a decision quickly. The walls were a good eight feet tall. So I went back for the step ladder and tip-toed past the cricket club house wondering if anybody was watching me. I found a small flat roof building at the corner of the stadium. Using the step ladder I climbed on the roof and sat on the edge and had a perfect view of the match. This messing around meant I missed the first goal by James Jennings. Wing back J J got an incredible first half hat-trick with some great left foot finishes.

Mid-way through the first half a nice lady with a Guiseley polo shirt opened a gate and enquired if I was a County fan. She said that Halifax fans the previous week had talked about viewing the match from the cricket field and they were being cautious with away fans.

After a nice chat I think the lady decided I was a genuine and un-threatening character and let me in. I collected my step ladder and entered the ground. I mentioned the book. The lady said – "don't mention anything about gaining a good view from outside the ground, just say you blagged your way in". I responded by explaining that the book will not be out for nine months. I thought to myself that the book may not even see the light of day but I better keep writing just in case. Thank you Trudi Hannaford for letting me in and your friendly hospitality.

The stadium is a nice, neat ground. Guiseley spent a couple of years in the National League so the ground was improved to meet that standard. I counted three fans other than the media and staff. Me and two Guiseley supporters. One fellow behind the goal who barked out complaints to the ref and another stood near me on the terrace along the side of the pitch. Nice chap and it transpired that normally he works on the gates. He reminded me that John Rooney and Ash Palmer are ex- Guiseley. He said they usually get good income from perennial pre-season friendlies against Leeds and Bradford but the pandemic has scuppered that. It reminded me of the effect that the loss of income will have on clubs like Guiseley.

County won 5-1 and we looked great. To be fair to Guiseley they had a couple of triallists who must have wondered what was happening as we put the opposition to the sword. We had about fifteen chances on target. Their goal was a good one. I nice breakaway and composed finish. Our other scorers were the ever-impressive John Rooney and another by Richie Bennett.

All in all, well worth the trip and I have a claim to "fame". I was the only County fan at a first team match.

In other news, the goalposts are moved once again with the size of crowds allowed into National League games. The National League have made an announcement that a maximum 1,000 fans will be allowed into stadiums at the start of the season on 3rd October. Seeing as County have sold 2,700 season tickets that causes a bit of a problem. The indication was that roughly 25% of stadium capacities will be allowed. Therefore the calculation of 2,700 at Edgeley Park. To be fair the National League did advise clubs not to sell season tickets until an announcement was made. Nevertheless, with the season less than three weeks away the National League have left it until the last minute to allow clubs to arrange tickets sales and confirm arrangements. Piss up and brewery come to mind.

We may have to put season ticket holders on a rota of matches or a ballot. Or hopefully County will convince the numpties at the National League that 2,700 is workable.

Wednesday 16th September

Another dark day in football. Recently Bury and now Macc. Macclesfield have been wound up in the High Court with debts totalling more than £500,000.

A lot of businesses and especially football clubs cannot sustain a gap in income for more than three months. The pandemic has been going on for six months. Even under normal circumstances football clubs are on the brink. They stumble along paying fees and wages they can barely afford. Or will never afford. A sad day for all Macc fans and football fans in general.

From my perspective, that means two less games this year and two local derbies gone.

Saturday 19th September 2020

York City 0 v County 1 (behind closed doors "secret" friendly) at Bootham Crescent

This one has been kept secret by both clubs. A shame for the York fans as this will be The Minstermen's last game at Bootham Crescent. There is a 10pm curfew in York for pubs and it appears that the club doesn't want fans to congregate around the ground or opposition fans to travel. York is a great city for pubs and drinking. There could be some trouble if the fans can't get in the ground. There is a rumour that the game may be on but no information from both clubs.

I made a couple of calls to York City. A fella picked up and put the phone down. Then I tried a few more times with no one answering. I was hoping to blag a press pass. York is about 83 miles from my house. Considering I wasn't sure of the kick-off time or whether we were actually playing York by 11:30am, I admitted defeat.

As predicted County did indeed play York. A 1pm kick-off. The club decided they wanted the game to pass unnoticed for security reasons. They didn't want their own fans gathering for the final game at their home since 1932. A real shame and the pandemic has ruled out a last goodbye for fans.

County registered a 1-0 win with an 86th minute goal from Nyal Bell. Our fifth straight pre-season victory. Highlights were available that evening featuring our dominance with two attempts hitting the post in the first minute. Further goal line clearances by York kept the score line down to one. County showed once again that they are a force to be reckoned with this season.

Things are shaping up rather well for the Hatters.

Tuesday 22nd September 2020

Chorley v County at Victory Park (behind closed doors friendly) - Cancelled

County go up the road into Lancashire to play Chorley in another pre-season friendly. A behind closed doors fixture which I need to find a way of attending. Knowing Victory Park quite well, I remember it would be impenetrable. Just to make sure, I paid a visit the week before. A full scout around the ground. As expected, I confirmed it's layout from a previous visit. This consists of a large stand adjacent to a park. Two sides where you would have to go through someone's back garden and sit on top of their garage to get a view of the pitch. In fact, there is only one way in through the main entrance on a small industrial estate.

Guiseley was quite an innocent blag. Scaling the stands of Victory Park or infiltrating a domestic back garden is not good form. Unperturbed I harked back to my gig reviewing days and thought I may as well blag a backstage pass or press pass. I walked into the office and asked if I could speak with someone who could consider me for a pass. Usually, you need accreditation. Luckily, I was directed to club secretary Graham Watkinson. I lovely chap who was happy to hear my book story. Non-league has a great spirit amongst its club staff and a love for the game. Graham said it would be no problem and asked me to send him an email and a pass would be sorted.

This put a spring in my step. I looked at Victory Park and admired the stadium. Decent for non-league. The sun was shining and I planned that weather permitting I would ride up next Tuesday on the Royal Enfield.

On the way home I nipped into Edgeley Park to see what the press pass situation was for the coming season. I had a chat with the ticket office manager and he had heard about my blag at Guiseley. He explained that the club photographer Mike Petch was the only member of staff with a pass. Due to Covid there was no plan at this stage to release any more. I was asked to send in an email to be kept updated.

I had bumped into Mike Petch at Guiseley. Mike mentioned that there were plans for an official County book this season. More of a photographic catalogue of the season compared to my memoir. After fifteen years as official photographer Mike was chuffed, that County were considering doing a book including his photos.

The weather was perfect for photos with a clear blue sky. I took a shot of the new cladding on the Cheadle End. I sneaked into the ground as the Pop side was open and took a couple of pics of the empty stadium. Visiting the loos inside the executive lounges it transpired that everything is in the process of being refurbished.

Unfortunately, the Chorley match got cancelled the day before it was supposed to be played. It was good to get the phantom press pass and thanks to the very hospitable folk at Chorley FC. Good experience too as it appears that if you walk into a non-league club and ask nicely, they will more than likely accommodate your request.

Not sure of the reason for the last-minute cancellation but Chorley have recorded consecutive 3-1 defeats in pre-season against lower league opposition. We have just smashed Guiseley 5-1 and recorded five wins on the bounce. Maybe the Magpies from Chorley thought their prep was not sufficient to counter the mighty Hatters.

Thursday 24th September- National League D Day (again)

This season gets more bizarre by the week. The first D Day was the points per game calculation of the finishing positions for last season. This was where County were in a play-off position and the form team but were replaced by Barnet in the play-offs.

This week the government has effectively delayed fans attending elite sport by six months. The National League is considered elite sport. Up until the spike in infections over the last few weeks, the National League was planned to start with approx. 25% of capacity in attendance in stadiums. This was downgraded to a maximum of a 1,000 last-week. Partial lockdowns are being introduced and it looks like the government is going to delay the attendance of fans at matches.

Today, the board of the National League consult with clubs to confirm-

- Does the season start a week on Saturday?
- Will there be any fans in the stadium?
- If so, will all matches be available live to stream by fans?
- Will this be subsidised?
- Are the government going to financially support the League?

These factors will dictate-

- How do all the season ticket holders get compensated for non-attendance?
- What financial effect will this have on the clubs?
- Will this mean that some clubs go to the wall?
- If so, what plans are there to work out points if clubs drop out and go bust?
- As a result will this affect promotion and relegation?
- Would there still be promotion and relegation?

Seeing as County are promotion favourites, hopefully we would still get promoted!

Clubs have already invested in bringing players back, pre-season training and matches, pitch and stadium prep. The clubs have set out their grounds to accommodate the Covid social distancing rules. In non- league, without fans in stadiums, many clubs will be on the brink of liquidation within six months.

There is uncertainty but the attraction of football club ownership continues. Burnley have American investment bankers courting them. More bizarrely our very own National League mates Wrexham have Hollywood stars looking to buy a bit of North Wales. Ryan Reynolds and Rob McElhenney are the stars in question.

Whether these American guys will spend any time in downtown Wrexham is unclear. It should be mandatory for owners to get down with the fans. I'm not sure if the hotel choices in central Wrexham are quite up to it though. It is likely that these dudes will drop in by helicopter and then retreat to a luxury country manor in the posh enclaves of Clwyd.

Football without fans is nothing. When the owners, managers and players move on the fans are still there. Through thick and thin. Through wind, rain, sleet, promotion and relegation. Travelling the length and breadth of the country often spending money they can't afford. Then, when the shit hits the fan and your club goes bust who picks up the pieces? The fans groups. Just look at Bury FC reborn as Bury AFC.

FA Cup winners with 135 years of history gone bust with no help from the football authorities. Reborn as Bury AFC. Starting again in the Northwest Counties League.

I mention FA Cup. When I was a kid the FA Cup was lauded like winning the First Division. Now, it has been relegated to a distraction on the road to qualifying for the Champions League. Rather than win a trophy the elite just want to finish fourth and fill their coffers full of TV cash. Forget trophies, let us just wallow in the corporate malaise and pay average players fortunes. While fans watch on TV and comment inanely on twitter. Rant over and feel free to call me an old git. I would sooner watch lower league football anyway.

The National League have held their meeting. They have issued a short statement of about two paragraphs. In an outdated font that harks back to the 90's or older. The detail is sketchy. It says something like "we don't know what we are really doing but we've asked for some dosh off the government so we don't get all the blame when some of our clubs go bust". They have not confirmed if the league starts next Saturday.

Reading between the lines it appears the government will assist financially and the season will start behind closed doors on the 3rd October. The financial assistance is rumoured to be about a third of the requested amount. But it looks like we kick off at three next Saturday. Oh well, let's see how many clubs finish the season then. I suppose that the worst off have a 33% chance of survival. Luckily, County will be OK.

Saturday 26th September 2020

County 2 v Kidderminster Harriers 1 at Edgeley Park (behind closed doors friendly)

The final pre-season friendly for County. Behind closed doors with no chance of getting in and our website states that fans outside will be moved along. I will watch this on the website but it comes as a bit of a relief as there are family duties this weekend. Eldest son Will travels to Uni on the Friday for his first day at Northumbria Uni in Newcastle. Then we travel up to Glasgow to see daughter Daniela who is studying up there. A double header of fatherly duty. It would have taken some explanation to squeeze in a pre-season friendly.

I am two out of two for possible matches up to now. So not bad considering. One of approximately 300 County fans at Colne and the lone Hatter at Guiseley. The pandemic is approaching the second wave. After a period of getting back to normal it looks like new lockdown measures. This will cramp my style in terms of attending matches. I will try to contact any clubs direct unless County come back to me about a potential press passes. First call will be to Torquay United for the first game of the season on the 3rd October. Not much chance but worth a call.

Football fan trials have been cancelled temporarily. There were trials of 1000 fans in grounds in the Football League and a pre-season friendly at Brighton. With the infection rate increasing and a 10pm curfew for pubs and restaurants, the government has abandoned the possibility of the return of fans in October.

As for our match up with the Harriers from the Black Country this one was viewed in a pub. We are up in Newcastle dropping the eldest lad off at Uni. How things have changed since the 80's with the comparable luxury that awaited us at the halls. Heating, cleanliness and all the mod cons. Any one old enough to go the same route in the 80's or even 70's will recall surroundings akin to the TV series Rising Damp. Or the Young Ones. Whereby typical student accommodation consisted of damp and smelly Victorian housing. I forged an alternative path to further education.

The family found a pub for the lunch time kick off for Brighton v United. Also the live stream of County on my phone. United somehow won the game with a penalty after the final whistle. The ball was in the air while a Brighton defender handled as the ref blew the whistle. I bizarre end to the match. The Premier League season has started with plenty of goals but plenty of pens as the hand ball rule has been tightened up.

Fans are fed up with VAR stoppages. Any contact with a hand in any bodily position in the box is now a pen. Typically with Premier League players, any slight contact in the box of any kind now becomes a pen. The players just throw themselves to the ground with the slightest brush. Sometimes when they could have easily carried on and probably scored. Another reason I prefer lower league football.

With my mobile phone propped up against a pint glass I watched the Hatters beat Kiddy 2-1. A John Rooney pen at the end of the first half. Then a cool finish at the end by Nyal Bell. Second game running for Nyal to score a late winner. Six of the best now as County completed six pre-season wins in a row. We didn't play as well as previous games but it has been an excellent pre-season.

I regaled the family with how good the Danny Bergara stand looks. New dugouts and advertising has tidied up the roof and front of the stand. New seats in the Railway End have been added. EP looks great and ready for the new season. The lads and Kath had a quick look and then instructed me to get more drinks in. I know my place.

CHAPTER TEN
October 2020

Saturday 3rd October 2020

Torquay United 1 v County 0 (first match of the season)

My memories of Torquay go way back to the 70's. My one match at Plainmoor was in 1977 when on holiday with my brother and grandparents. I recall it was a Friday night and must have been one of the first games of the season. It was when Elvis died so was somewhere around the 16th August '77.

Being football nuts we would seek out matches where possible. When my Granddad was not watching United at home, we would visit local sides. I recall Oldham, Altrincham and County of course. An Oldham match had something in common with Torquay as we experienced football aggro. This was the 70's after all. At Plainmoor we stood on an open terrace behind the goal. Still hot at night on the English Riviera, the sparsely populated terrace provided a chilled-out perch to watch the match. At half time it kicked off. Me and my brother were quite entertained by a group of skinheads fighting each other. I'm not sure whether it was Torquay fans or even anything to do with football. Being young and naïve I was not particularly scared by the incident which was over in a flash.

At Oldham it was more sinister. A few years later around 1980 the same crew – me, my brother and Granddad went to ice station zebra or Boundary Park as it is officially known. This was in mid- winter and it was brass monkeys. A complete contrast to the English Riviera. The Latics were playing Chelsea in the old Second Division. We went in a paddock opposite the main stand. Little did we know that the seats above us housed the Chelsea "fans". The paddock was almost empty but a barrage of coins and pies rained down from above.

Fortunately, we stood right against the wall at the back of the paddock. This spot protected us from the trajectory of the missiles from above. More Oldham fans came into the paddock and an exchange of chants ensued. I remember hearing London accents for the first time swearing. Genuinely scary as Chelsea fans got into the paddock. Only the arrival of the constabulary quelled the violence. I am a pacifist so this aggro stuff has been purely observational over the years.

After taking what seemed like two days to travel from Stockport to Devon, we ramped up at our caravan site in Torquay. My flat-footed Granddad had obliterated the clutch on the maroon-coloured Ford Escort estate. Relief on arrival was akin to the American pioneers finally reaching their destination out west in their wagon trains.

After collecting our caravan key we navigated our way through rows of brand-new caravans. In the centre of the site was a small gathering of turd brown and cream painted caravans. Straight out of the 1950's. One was ours. After the initial shock we had a cracking holiday. There was a heatwave and we watched Torquay at Plainmoor.

On to our 2020 fixture versus The Gulls. This is the first match of the season. After a great pre-season County are well up for it. The bizarre lockdown situation has prevented fans from attending matches. I have done my best in pursuit of the initial theme of the book. To attend as many fixtures as possible. Lockdown has pitched a curve ball at my ambitions but also added a unique theme to the season.

In the week building up to the game lockdown seems to be getting stricter. I sent a couple of emails to the Torquay media and press officers. I had an automated reply from one saying that "due to no upcoming first team fixtures I am temporarily away from the ground and will get back to you if the situation changes". This was not very promising. I awaited a reply from the other contact.

I must admit it may not be the end of the world if I watch this match on the live stream. Travel involves a journey of approximately four and half to five-hours by car. Plus, I would need to do the return journey. Taking the missus to the English Riviera was an option with an overnight stay. But Jonnie needs to get to his football on Sunday morning.

I have seen County play at Hartlepool, Southampton and various long-distance destinations over the years. Involving past midnight return home times with work the same morning. Us footy fans love this dedicated activity. I have done those journeys on coaches and driving a twenty-year-old Ford Escort. On one occasion coming back from a match in Blackpool aboard the Escort, the headlights failed. Then the hole beneath my feet near the peddles expanded letting in a spray of dirty water for the journey back to Cheshire.

Attendance at Torquay is scuppered as the second contact confirmed that he was interested in my book but entry is not possible. No passes available and I think this will be the theme from the National League clubs with the current lockdown. I have toyed with contacting the Manchester Evening News and volunteering to cover the matches. However, I believe that Sam Byrne of the Stockport Express is "syndicated" to provide reports for the MEN too.

Anyway, I want to keep this independent and anecdotal. It is what it is and the live streams seem the best way forward until I can gain entry via tickets or blag my way in. I am also conscious that I don't want to be flouting lockdown rules. Being a 53-year-old "responsible" adult and all that. Strange days indeed.

It has been announced that County season tickets holders will get all the home games streamed with no charge. £7.50 for non-season tickets holders which is decent value. It looks like we won't be back in the stadium until the end of November at best. Torquay are steaming this away match at

£9.00. Damned cheaper than travelling down there. If the presentation is up to our standard, I will be more than happy.

Typical County, we dominated the game and lost 1-0 to a goal in injury time. We battered them. Last year the result ended up 5-1 to the Hatters. On that occasion we caught them on the counter-attack. This time they caught us with a sucker punch in the last minute. To be fair The Gulls manager Gary Johnson made a triple substitution that changed the game in midfield. Up until that point midway through the second half we should have already scored three or four. A combination of goal line clearances and less than ruthless finishing thwarted us.

We look a classy team but we miss a finisher up front. Richie Bennett is a good hold up man. He had a couple of good chances. One should have been the winner. A tame shot when more power would have slotted the ball past the keeper. We need a man to play off Richie. Nyal Bell is not really that player being a big fella and more of a like for like replacement from the bench. Food for thought for Jim.

It was good to watch the stream with the opposition commentary team in action. Usually the perspective is from our commentators. The Gulls men at the microphone were impartial and praised the Hatters describing the Gulls victory as smash and grab. Our domination was described as like a siege at the Alamo. Three points dropped then.

Plainmoor looked pretty good and you really get a good view of the stands when empty. It was interesting to hear the Torquay anecdotes about players of old. Torquay have not had much to shout about over the decades with their dog bite incident about the only story of note. This was when one of their players was bitten by a police dog on the pitch in the 80's. This delayed a crucial last game of the season. The delay helped, Torquay got a last-minute winner and beat Crewe 3-2. Otherwise they would have dropped out of the football league.

It is hard enough supporting County at times but easier than following the Gulls. Torquay have had the odd cup highlight.

Other than that and the dog bite it has been a barren history. At least we have had several Wembley visits and exciting promotions up to the second tier of the Football League. Some lower league clubs rely on the loyalty of the fans without any success. Next up Halifax.

Tuesday 6th October 2020
County 2 v FC Halifax Town 1

Here we are back at Edgeley Park. Season tickets renewed. EP is resplendent in new cladding. A pre-season make-over courtesy of our generous new owners. But wait a minute, where are we? Yes, this looks familiar. Blooming 'eck, it's my living room and we are watching on the telly. My brand-new season ticket pass via the County website stream.

It would have been much better live in the ground but this is the bizarre 2020 reality. A year ago you would have been laughed at for suggesting there will be a global pandemic and matches will be played behind closed doors. United would lose 6-1 to Spurs and Villa will beat Liverpool 7-2. Yes, the world has gone mad and football has too.

One minor gripe to get out of the way though before the football starts. The name of Halifax. I still think of the Shaymen as Halifax Town. Unfortunately for the West Yorkshiremen they went bust about ten years ago. This necessitates the creation of a new company with a slightly different name. Now they are pre-fixed FC Halifax Town. Very continental like FC Barcelona. Why not just Halifax Town AFC or something more English? Worse still is FCUM or Football Club United of Manchester. They are based in North Manchester not the Catalan region.

I suppose the marketing managers need to earn their corn. In the case of FCUM though the formation of an alternative United for disenfranchised fans always puzzled me. I get the fact big United have departed somewhat from the fan experience of the 70's and 80's. I understand that the current owners are probably undesirable. However, the whole of the Premier League have gone down that route. A more sanitised and corporate stadium environment with overseas and often nefarious owners.

If all fans decided to form a new version of their club a whole new league would need to be set up. The disenfranchised former Premiership team supporters league. Besides, why didn't the FCUM fans just go and support their local lower league side? Say Macclesfield or Bury for example. They certainly could have done with their help.

What happened at County v the Shaymen? The match could be described as a talented new team full of team spirit (County) versus an old school tactical unit. Halifax were well drilled, tough and determined. They let us play in their own half then hunted us down once County crossed the halfway line. The Hatters dominated the first half then got frustrated and sloppy in the second half.

Proceedings were not helped by the omission of our captain Hogan. Apparently, Hogan and Nyal Bell had a confrontation at the end of the Torquay defeat last week. Jim Gannon dropped both players. Sam Minihan, great at full back, was moved more central to compensate for the missing Hogan. This unbalanced the defence and caused us problems.

Despite the line-up change we played OK and worked hard as a unit. Team spirit is good and substitute Adam Thomas came on to score a "worldy" of a winner. A left foot rocket that nearly broke the net. A 2-1 victory and great for morale. We are off the mark points wise and another three at home to Dover on Saturday will represent a good start to the season.

The first goal was worth noting. A fine move which led to a left foot shot by Mark Kitching nestling nicely in the Shaymen's onion bag. Adam Thomas got man of the match for his brilliant goal but Mark Kitching was the stand-out County player overall. Full of running, the lad never stopped and looks to have cemented a first team place.

Checking twitter I tried to figure out who was there. Oliver Holt the Stockport County supporting journalist was there. Mark Stott our new owner was in attendance. Sam Byrne from the Stockport Express will have been there along with Mike

Petch our photographer. Jon Keighren was commentating along with Chris Ridgway the County supporting boxing journalist. There was a splattering of people in the exec seats- probably directors from Halifax and County. Plus the subs social distancing above the dugouts in the seats where Jonnie and I should be sitting.

Special mention goes to Akito Aoki who was watching in the middle of the night from Japan. Jon Keighren gave the Samurai Hatter a nice name check in the commentary. So, a satisfactory first home match of the season. It is great to be back and it will be even better when I can get back into my seat in the ground.

Saturday 10th October 2020

County 3 v Dover Athletic 0

Dover is 295 miles from Stockport and 27 miles from Calais. I realise the 27 miles is pretty much water but I thought I would highlight the distance. If we are allowed back into grounds by the 8th May 2021, I will be visiting Dover for the away fixture. I cannot travel three miles to EP today but I will be travelling at least five hours (probably over six hours) and 295 miles next May. I thought I would just put that bit of craziness out there. I am presuming that this pandemic and lockdown stuff will be over by then. God help us if it's not. I am hoping we will be allowed back into the stadiums by the end of November. Besides, by May 2021 with good play and luck in our sails, County may even be promoted. My glass is always half full.

Just a little bit about Dover. Formed in 1983, they climbed up the non-league pyramid quickly and then dropped back down only to rise-up again. Although they probably have a decent catchment area for fans, they will always be up against it financially and reliant on loyalists through the turnstiles. Due to their location most matches will be a long-distance journey adding more pressure to the bank balance.

Their chairman recently announced that the longer the fan ban goes on, the more likely the chance that his club will go bust. The danger being that County could be playing matches that may be annulled before the end of the season. Macclesfield have already gone bust with their fixtures now removed from the National League programme.

This puts this whole pandemic situation into stark reality for clubs at our level. In fact all levels are not immune from these financial pressures. With optimism at County in full flow we have found a remedy of sorts with our new owners.

Talking of hopefully travelling all the way to Dover and back, I discovered an amazing Hatters website. I found the website 57hattersyears.co.uk through twitter. The site logs decades of home and away match reports. I have never been that active on social media but have promoted my classic album tracks radio show occasionally on Facebook and twitter. Apparently, the social media platforms have algorithms. This is a computer process which predicts your interests. It sounds a bit big brother but leads you to interesting sites.

Since writing this blog, the positive effect of social media is that twitter seems to have highlighted loads of County tweets. I've posted a few photos from pre-season and the twitter "computer" has decided I should be "given" loads of County content. Cool. Through this, 57 Hatters Years popped up from County fanatic Martin Frost. An amazing log of attending nearly 2000 matches. 850 of which were away games.

County's yo-yo existence has taken the club up and down through five divisions meaning Martin has visited nearly all the ninety-two traditional league clubs. Plus all the non-league ones from our recent history. Brilliantly compiled the website is an inspiration. It is heart-warming to read similar anecdotes about the County watching experience over the decades.

On to the match itself, County disposed of Dover efficiently in the end. The Whites manager Andy Hessenthaler set them up for a draw, got ten men behind the ball and frustrated County in the first half. Captain Hogan returned after serving his time for his discretion at Torquay to bolster the Hatters defence. This allowed Minihan back into his right-wing back position and Sam had a great game. At half time Jim Gannon made another good substitution with Alex Reid replacing Connor Jennings.

Reid provided more movement up front playing off the ever-reliable Richie Bennett. County started to open the Dover defence and their keeper brought down Reid and John Rooney duly dispatched the penalty. Reid scored off a good Richie Bennett lay off and then Rooney completed the scoring in the last minute from close range. Solid performance with standouts being Reid, Rooney, Bennett and Minihan. This victory elevated County to joint fourth in the table.

In other news Kai, the nephew of John Rooney got two goals for the County under 11's today. Hope he is as good as Wayne or John. Plus the club strengthened their scouting team this week by recruiting three new regional scouts including Matt Jansen the ex- Blackburn Rovers and Bolton player.

Tuesday 13th October 2020

Wealdstone 2 v County 5

Wealdstone is one of those places that is part of the outer urban sprawl between Watford and Uxbridge in Northwest London. Not far from Wembley. I have worked around there several times over the years involved in construction sites. Without being too unkind it is bland and run down in some areas. They used to say it is grim up north but I would describe it as grim down south around northwest London. Travelling with work has been an ideal opportunity to combine work and mid-week matches. But I have never been to Wealdstone for a match and County have never played them. The ground is in Ruislip which might be one of the nice bits so apologies to any Ruislipians.

I scouted out Grosvenor Vale on Google maps and it looks about as impenetrable as possible. Hemmed in on three sides by houses and with only one way in through the front gate. Shame as some of the perimeter walls look low so I was contemplating doing a "Guisley". Wealdstone is where Stuart Pearce and Vinny Jones started their careers. I had a vision of Stuart and Vinny manning the gates ready to eject any northern blaggers writing season reviews. They could be ably assisted by the Wealdstone raider their semi-famous fan known for enquiring if opposition fans "want some".

I made the standard perfunctory press pass request. This was emailed to the media officer and their general enquiry email. It looks like we are going in to further lock down measures later this week so I didn't hold much hope for a positive response. I think in general clubs will only accommodate the minimum possible people while this covid malarkey continues. I did get a polite rejection from Torquay but I thought that Wealdstone may be a good litmus test. Torquay like County are essentially a football league set up. They are less likely to accommodate random book writers like me. While Wealdstone are your traditional non-leaguers. Their grounds are local social clubs and community set ups. They are true non-league and may be more accommodating.

Alas, on this occasion it will be the live stream for me. I got a quick response from the Wealdstone club secretary Paul Fruin. A standard type response- "Due to the strict Covid Guidelines with behind closed doors games we are only accepting media requests from official club media and league partners."

This response will be de rigueur for clubs until the government decides fans are allowed back in grounds. I have had the same response from the bigger clubs and the traditional non-league type clubs. No big surprise but at least I have tried. The lifesaver being that all the clubs are going to live stream the matches. Wealdstone is £9.99. National League clubs feature live on TV only once or twice a season. So the only upside to the pandemic is that we get to see all the matches live albeit on the streams. In the past if you wanted to see our away matches live you had to travel. Or just listen on the radio until highlights were available.

The Wealdstone stream was like tuning in to a second world war BBC broadcast. The sound in parts was akin to a Norman Collier broken microphone routine. The visuals were closer to a slide show as the stream froze intermittently. Fortunately, most of the match was watchable and none of the seven goals were missed. County stuffed the Stones 5-2 in the drizzle of northwest London. I told you it was grim down south.

Rooney scored a hat-trick. Another penalty and two other composed finishes. John is clearly a class above in this league and the game changer in this match. It was not plain sailing as Wealdstone went ahead twice before County out classed them in the second half. There was frustration for two thirds of the match as we wasted an avalanche of corners. Bennett scored a great finish and after the match I counted that he also had three assists. Richie may not be the most prolific goal-scorer but he adds a lot to this team. Jim will be more than happy with the result. However, he will want more from set pieces and a more ruthless return from chances created.

County are now up to second in the table. We are scoring lots of goals with the look of a team that should be right up there in the top three at the end of the campaign, if not top. Next up we travel to Chesterfield which will be a sterner test than the Stones.

In other news, two developments at either end of the football spectrum have occurred. The first being a great development for Macc. Moss Rose has been purchased by a local businessman. The ground was on Right Move the online estate agent. That is a scary nadir when your ground goes on a day-to-day house buying site.

A "saviour" has been found. I use the word saviour with caution as County and lots of clubs have had so called saviours over the years. Worryingly, the Macc press conference with the new group of saviours had one or two dodgy looking characters sat at the table. It reminded me of the press conferences we had with the dodgy charlatans involved in our club in the past. The saving grace may be Robbie Savage who is part of the Macc consortium. He lives in Macc and seems to be a decent fella. Macclesfield FC will now apply for a place in the Northwest Counties league.

Talking of dodgy consortiums the top six clubs in the Premier League have come up with a "project big picture." This is a plan for the top six clubs to have more control than the rest of their league. Then to kick two teams out and make the Prem an eighteen-team competition. They have promised to give 25% of the TV revenue to the EPL. That bit sound promising. However most fans smell a rat.

Liverpool and Man United are heading up the proposals. The cynic may suggest that because of reduced incomes recently they see an opportunity to fast track their power over football. Throw some bait while times are hard and do a power grab. I have an affinity for United but every United fan I have spoken with do not support the "project big picture" proposals.

Fortunately for the rest of the Premier league teams, this proposal is unlikely to happen. After all, why would turkeys vote for Christmas.

Saturday 17thth October 2020
Chesterfield 1 v County 2

This one is live on the telly. Yes, County on live TV. Back in the glory days of 96/97 and our magnificent promotion and run to the League Cup semi-final, County were regulars on the reels of regional and national highlights packages. We soon faded from national prominence but for a brief-moment in football history we were news. County should have had even more coverage in the previous Danny Bergara era. We visited Wembley on multiple occasions and battled for promotion regularly. In that period for some reason Granada TV seemed to favour the likes of Tranmere. I cannot remember why. Maybe Elton Welsby favoured the Merseyside clubs.

At the end of the glorious 96/97 season County confirmed promotion away at Chesterfield. At their old Saltergate ground. Tonight the Hatters play the Spireites at their new flatpack arena – The Technique Stadium. If you took a poll of proper hard-core fans, I would predict that 80% would prefer their old ground over a new identikit stadium. Saltergate was old, in need of a good lick of paint and new toilets. Or any toilets fit for modern hygiene. Some TLC was required. But it had character and history and a traditional location near where people live.

These new grounds are all the same. On the edge of town or in a retail park. No traditional pubs nearby and surrounded by the same bland retail units. The stands are boxy, plain with no discernible character. We will end up like America. Driving to the edge of town arenas with no pubs and the only option being to hold tail-gate parties.

I do hold judgement for the very occasional exception. The new Brentford stadium has some individuality and design credibility. Chesterfield is the alternative. Practical and bland. Nice enough I suppose if you have not experienced anything different.

Today, County went to the top of the league with a fourth win on the bounce. Our highest league position since 2011. Chesterfield were tough with a very annoying centre forward. Tom Denton the 6 ft 6in journeyman. Basically, you can pump the ball up to him and he is going to knock the ball on creating panic in a defence. That was Chesterfields tactic. County were far the better footballing side but had to scrap for the victory.

Kitching supplied our opener cutting in and directing a great shot into the net from his weaker right foot. A mirror image to the Adam Thomas goal against Halifax. Jim again made some inspired subs with Alex Reid scoring the winner. A composed header after a flurry of shots at the Chesterfield goal.

Another spirited performance. Standouts today were the ever-consistent Minihan, tireless Bennett, relentless Hogan, energetic Kitching and composed Reid. This squad has a collective desire to win. A team led by a top manager. The back-room staff and overall set up are working well. The investment from Mr Stott is already paying off.

County are at the top of the table even though challengers Hartlepool have a game in hand. Jim Gannon and County are known for coming strong in the second half of the season. This early season run bodes well if we can keep up the consistency throughout the league campaign. Next up, the FA Cup at home to today's hosts Chesterfield.

Saturday 24th October 2020
FA Cup Fourth Round Qualifying
County 1 v Chesterfield 1 (lost 6-7 on pens)

Inspired by victory over the Spireites, County continue their campaign in the FA Cup hoping to repeat last Saturdays victory against the same opposition. Will this be a chance for Jim to change the team around giving some game time to the likes of Croasdale, Bell and Williams?

As I write this, we have just entered tier three. Not the team, we are still in tier five unfortunately. Tier three of lockdown for 28 days. This is a disputed imposition as far as most Stopfordians are concerned. Tier three is for Greater Manchester. We are in Cheshire. Or we consider ourselves Cheshire as we have been ignoring the 1974 civic reconfiguration dumping Stocky into Mancunia. I grew up in Hazel Grove in the first ten years of my life which is nearer Macclesfield than Moston. The Grove borders Poynton which is still in Cheshire.

Rather naively I thought earlier in the week that if a pub serves substantial meals, I can just go in and drink. I have since had it confirmed that alcohol is only served if you have a substantial meal. This severely cramps ones pub going style so it looks like we are confined to barracks for today's FA Cup clash. There were a few pubs in Stockport showing the match on big screens but it looks like most will be watching from home today.

After all, ordering a substantial meal with every batch of alcohol sounds a bit of a pain in the derriere. Can you order chicken and chips and four pints or is it only a reasonable number of drinks per substantial meal? By the time you've put a face mask on for every slash (and I am a regular slasher) the whole thing sounds crap. So for me, viewing the match is on the telly in my house with as many beers as I like and I can visit the bog mask free. Nice one.

I have signed two petitions this last week or so. A football supporter petition for a debate in parliament to get fans back in grounds. This petition needed over 100,000 signatures which it got. The government message back was underwhelming. It was along the lines of cheers; you will get your debate but don't hold too much hope as we are in the middle of a pandemic. Even though there is a massive positive argument for controlled outdoor events which will improve the mental health of loads of people.

The other petition was for no public money for MPs' meal's. As you may know, MPs have a heavily subsidised bar and canteen. So you can imagine plenty of scotch and gin guzzled at 1970's prices. Their canteen is probably M & S/ Waitrose standard at minimum if not some top London catering scran. Compare this to families who need free school meals and it becomes a bit of a scandal. Fair play to Marcus Rashford for highlighting the issue.

Before the action I need to mention my new lucky shirt. During the summer I purchased a retro shirt. Like the 1967 Division. Four champions shirt. Blue cotton etc but with a County badge from the 80's. Bit of a hybrid but very tasty (as shirts go). I have worn this for the last four matches and we have won all four. Jonnie has been wearing his 13/14 blue home shirt. But he is switching to the new white away shirt today. I am not particularly superstitious but I thought I would mention it.

While in the club shop recently, I nearly bought the new fluorescent yellow away top. But I have a policy these days that I don't buy nylon material shirts. I have a nylon 1978

Bukta home shirt. Unfortunately, even if you are slightly overweight non-cotton footy shirts are not the best look. Plus my missus claims that middle aged men in football shirts should be given a custodial sentence.

County only made one change with Reid starting instead of Connor Jennings. Bell did come on for Bennett and Croasdale came on right at the end for his first action of the season. Hogan scored our goal. In a rather frustrating match, County failed to capitalise on taking the lead. We had a few chances to put the game to bed. In torrential rain, the Spireites scored in the last few minutes forcing a penalty shoot-out.

Our keeper Ben Hinchliffe scored one of our pens but we ended up losing 6-7. Probably our worst performance of the season so far. We were the better team overall but Chesterfield were typically dogged. A Cup run is always nice but as the saying goes; we can now concentrate on the league.

Tuesday 27thth October 2020

County 0 v 0 Solihull Moors

The Hatters look for a fifth straight league win against Solihull. Only formed in 2007 as a merger of Moor Green and Solihull Borough, Moors finished second in the National League in 2018/19. Managed by ex-County keeper Tim Flowers, Solihull lost to Fylde in the play-off semi-finals. Last season was less successful with a ninth placed finish and Flowers was replaced by former West Brom coach and Kidderminster manager Jimmy Shan.

We are currently having our best start to a league campaign since 93/94. It is a bummer that we cannot attend the matches in this great run. Especially for me, as I decided to write this book about it. However, these strange times have added a bit of extra content and perspective. One thing is for sure, these are good times to support County. After all the years of hurt we eventually tasted glory as champions of the National League North two seasons ago. Last season was decent in a pandemic shortened campaign. With our run of form, we may have got into the play-offs. Barnet scuppered us on the point per game rule.

Who would have thought less than twelve months ago that we would have a football season stopped early and then something called points per game introduced? Let alone a global pandemic. Bizarre times. Football supporters are hardy humans and I am sure attendances will return to their normal levels as soon as we get over this debacle.

On to the match, County have only beaten Moors once in eight attempts with five defeats. That record qualifies Solihull as a bogey team. County are a different proposition this season and firm favourites tonight. Undeterred by defeat against Chesterfield in the cup, I am persisting with the blue 67 County top. Seeing as I was born in 67 and we were Fourth Division champions in 67 I am convinced that we are due another glory year.

Ash Palmer, Maynard and Kitching are out through illness or injury. Moors have a few out too. Jack Prince is co-commentator tonight with Jon Keighren. Jack is the drummer with Wirral rock band the Coral. Jack should be drumming on tour in South America but is at a chilly Edgeley Park instead. The Coral are no strangers to our beloved ground as they played live at EP in front of about 20,000 last year with local band Blossoms. As a result, Evertonian Jack has a soft spot for the Hatters. Jack is also a UEFA B licensed coach and spent the summer coaching the Espanyol youngsters in Barcelona.

Rock music is my other passion. You may recall I have already plugged my radio show. Music and football tend to go hand in hand in the football mad Northwest. Most band members support football teams around these parts. Blossoms include a County fan. Unfortunately, they contain blues from Manchester too but no band is perfect. A perfect Saturday for me is to watch County win and then see a band in one of the pubs in Stockport.

Edgeley Park looks good and the tarpaulin has been removed from the Railway End exposing rather nifty new seats. The big scarf flag has found a new home at the back of the Railway End having been moved from its spiritual home in the Cheadle End.

Man of the match Ryan Croasdale came in for his first start. Both sets of players put a massive shift in. For a 0-0 draw it was entertaining action with both teams showing why they are promotion candidates. County had the better chances with two coming off the woodwork. The Hatters had twelve corners. An absorbing game that leaves County in second dropping one place and being replaced by Torquay who we should have beat on the opening day of the season. If we can collect three points against Weymouth at home on Saturday this will turn into a good point gained.

Saturday 31st October 2020

County 1 v Weymouth 2

The County boys play sunny Weymouth at the citadel of Cheshire football, Edgeley Park. Based way down on the Dorset coast the Terras nickname allegedly comes from their terracotta strip. That must have been their original kit as they don claret and blue these days. This lot are the most southernly based team apart from Torquay and I hope to visit them for our away fixture on 6th March 2021. Subject to the disappearance of the pandemic. Weymouth is 258 miles away or 516 miles there and back. However, by then I hope to be attending every possible match and more than happy to make the long haul to Dorset.

Long hauls are a badge of honour for us footy nutters. I have covered the north, southeast and midlands extensively with multiple away visits to most of County's opponents over the years. The south coast is a connoisseurs destination. London is relatively easy by train to most of the grounds.

Going past Bristol gets into tricky territory logistically. Multiple train changes resulting in expensive and time-consuming fanaticism. The only option is to hit the road. By coach or car or even motorbike. However, even a seasoned motor-biker like me doesn't look forward to six hours in the saddle to Dorset. Unless you make it into a longer trip over a few days.

Below I offer some anecdotes of southwest / south coast away travel. Even though this is a home game I hope to report on the actual journey in March. Off the top of my head I can dredge up several visits.

- Bristol Rovers- I have seen County at different grounds for this one. A 1-1 when Rovers temporarily played at Bath and another one at the Memorial ground in Bristol. I know a few Gas fans through work so a nice bit of banter was had with them.

- Salisbury- this was one of my random away matches but when Altrincham played there on a Tuesday night. Sometimes while away with work I would take in a match.

- Torquay- as mentioned earlier this was my only visit to Plainmoor in 1977 on summer holiday as a kid for an early season Friday night fixture. Can't remember the opposition but it wasn't County.

- Yeovil- a boring game watching County on a journey that seemed never ending but which is closer than Weymouth. The kind of game that makes you promise yourself that you will not be attending such games in the future. But as soon as the Hatters get on a good run you start looking at the fixtures and contemplate doing it all over again.

- Southampton- then there are the games that make it all worth-while; a visit to The Dell in the 96/97 League Cup run when County stunned the Saints 2-1 at the Dell in the quarter-final.

On to today's game at EP in the National League. County aim to continue an excellent start to the season and bag three points with a potential return to the top of the league. Weymouth meanwhile will be content with survival in this division. The Terras are still a part-time set up and that takes its toll over a long season at this level. County were still part-time last season and did well to finish eighth. We were the form team when the pandemic struck. If it were not for the points per game calculation, we would have been in a play-off position.

The Hatters are now full-time and beneficiaries of extra funding from our new County supporting owners. The additions to the squad have come up trumps in this opening month of the campaign. Weymouth at home must be a three-point haul if we have designs on automatic promotion or a play-off spot. Lose these types of games and they come back to haunt you at the business end of the season.

One point at home to Solihull is OK against a potential promotion rival. Supplemented by three points today and we are on course. Drop points and we lose momentum at the top. There are at least four key challengers this season- Sutton, Hartlepool, Notts County and Torquay. The most ruthless team will be champions. The rest may be in the play-offs. Of course there is always a surprise package but this is the likely scenario.

Prior to the game County have brought another player in. Forward Louis Britton comes in on loan from Bristol City. Louis was on loan at Torquay and was impressive coming on as a sub in our season opener against the Gulls. I will be doing a double header of National League action today. Following County's match Hartlepool v Torquay are live on BT Sports. Table topping Torquay play unbeaten Hartlepool who are fourth. This is an interesting one to gauge two of our key rivals for the title.

For today's match we have Palmer, Maynard and Kitching back with Croasdale deservedly retaining his place after a masterful midfield display on Tuesday. Ash Palmer makes his 100th County appearance and Ben Hinchcliffe his 200th. Both stalwarts over the last few years. New loanee Louis Britton is on the bench. United and England legend Nobby Stiles passed away yesterday. His great grandson provided the Remembrance Day reveille on the bugle before kick-off at Edgeley Park.

Weymouth line up 4-5-1 in what appears to be a damage limitation formation. County took the lead with a back-post header by an unmarked Ash Palmer from a corner. Dominating the first half, County go into the break at 1-0 and back on top of the table.

It is Halloween and the second half turned into a horror show. Like Wealdstone recently this is our first competitive match against the suitably nicknamed Terras. They certainly were a terror in the second half of this Halloween fixture. Like a team possessed Weymouth scored two breakaway goals. County didn't play badly in the second half but we couldn't convert our chances. As I said earlier the champions will be ruthless. County certainly have the quality but we need a ruthless streak.

As Halloween plays out and the country goes into a month-long full lockdown County nestle second in the table. The first month of the season ends with Torquay on top five points clear of the Hatters having played the same games. Indeed Torquay were ruthless in their televised match at Hartlepool. Three chances in the first half, ruthlessly converted for a 3-0 half time advantage. 5-0 at full time.

Not a bad start for us but could have been better. One point in the last two consecutive home league games has produced a stutter in our momentum. Our next match is in eleven days away at Notts County, one of three away matches as we go on the road in November. Sandwiched in between is a home fixture against a decent Eastleigh side.

Considering we have lost two and drawn one of the last three games I am sure Jim Gannon will use the next week or so to galvanize the players. The other defeat was on pens in the FA Cup against Chesterfield. The priority is the league but nevertheless we need to get back to winning ways. November is a big month for this group of players. No panic as far as I am concerned but hopefully, we will look back on this as a mere blip on the journey.

CHAPTER ELEVEN
November 2020

Wednesday 4th November 2020- FA Cup Fourth Round Qualifying (Replayed match)
County 4 v Chesterfield 0

In a season of bizarre circumstances, things just got stranger. On Monday 2nd November County are licking their wounds with over a week to go until the next match. Or maybe not. News comes through that we are in fact replaying our Chesterfield cup tie on Wednesday night. The Spireites were found guilty of fielding an ineligible player in the original game by the FA. Good news. But surely Chesterfield should be kicked out? Apparently, they have form for this and had the same situation after a Cup tie with MK Dons a few years ago. The current rules are that you must replay the match.

In an already congested season due to the pandemic, County now play tonight and if victorious Rochdale in the next round on Saturday. Is this good or bad? Are some of the players in need of a rest? In theory a break would have been good until next Wednesday. Now we have tonight, potentially an away tie at League 1 Rochdale on Saturday then a tough away match at Notts next Wednesday.

There have been a few negative rumblings from County fans this week. The performance against Weymouth wasn't great. We need to be patient as the team gels. We are still second and the squad is one of the best if not the best in the league. My one concern is the number of goals from our strikers. But let's keep the faith.

In more positive news from our ubiquitous owner Mark Stott, another great initiative was announced this week. The club have launched the food for Christmas campaign to fund school meals in holiday time in Stockport. The aim is to raise £220,000 and Mark Stott has personally donated £100,000. The government have been slow to support school meals in holiday time during the pandemic. So, up yours Boris.

To the match and do I really have to see Tom Denton of Chesterfield again? OK, we have them back at home in the league but four times in a season (if he's fit for the home league game). Tall, physical, cumbersome. A pain in the arse. Fortunately, County turned up big style.

In the first half the Hatters had a zip and purpose about them as good or better than any match this season. Jordan Keane was in for a start with Jennings, Bennett and Reid on for an attacking line up.

Within three minutes Rooney provided good control in the box feeding Bennett for an overhead kick into the net. Prepared to eat my words regarding our strikers Reid broke away and calmly slotted home for our second. Connor Jennings was good with County keeper Ben Hinchliffe a mere spectator. Very impressive.

The second half was more even with County benefitting from a somewhat fortuitous penalty. What looked like a borderline hand ball was given by the ref. Rooney duly converted exorcising his penalty miss in the previous cup match with the Spireites.

Then fifteen minutes later Reid is tripped just inside the box. Rooney converts again and it is 4-0. My mate Tom Denton fails to score against County again even-though he has scored in almost every match since January. Plus he handled the ball for our first pen. I don't mind Tom really.

Even with the way we played tonight, victory against Dale on Saturday would be considered a brilliant result.

Two leagues higher, Rochdale should be the favourites but I can see a very close encounter. Clearly, this squad is above National League level and let's hope we carry this momentum forward.

Saturday 7th November 2020- FA Cup First Round
Rochdale 1 v County 2

I rode past Spotland yesterday on the Royal Enfield. As an essential worker I can move around and have an exemption letter just in case I am stopped. I was at a site over in Lancashire and took the scenic route back over the hills dropping into Rochdale through Norden. Dale's ground lies just through Norden and is in a pleasant location dropping in from that direction. Nicer than coming through the town centre from the M60.

The spotlights are traditional and can be seen from some distance. Footy fans of an older vintage miss the lights. Back in the days before sat nav, grounds had these old type spotlights. The pylons were the travelling fans homing beacon. Often visible from several miles away they provided a comforting and exciting landmark especially when lit up. Spotland is a compact ground refurbished in the 90's and has a similar capacity to Edgeley Park. I took a quick diversion and circled around the ground for a look. I've been there to watch County a few times. Today would have provided a great away day with around 3,000 County supporters equalling the homes fan numbers.

Unfortunately, the ground will be empty apart from the teams and essential staff. Dale have been in League 1 for eight out of the last ten years. A brilliant performance considering their home attendances which average around 3,500. That figure includes some big away followings in League 1. Rochdale have found a successful formula at that level in spite of severe financial restrictions compared to their opposition. After spending a record thirty-six consecutive years in the bottom division from 1974 to 2010, Dale have progressed well.

County threatened Rochdale for that thirty-six-year record in the 70's and 80's. The Hatters spent twenty-two consecutive years in the bottom division before the Danny Bergara revolution. Now it is time for County to get back up to where they belong in League 1. When we get there, we need a solid plan and financial security making use of our solid support. We would be up at around 6,000 home crowds and more if we do well at that level.

On to today's FA cup tie. Richie Bennett is out as he has been in contact with someone who has contracted covid. A sensible precaution. Connor Jennings replaces Richie upfront alongside Alex Reid. Kitching returns and Jordan Keane makes his hundredth appearance. Ex- County player Jim McNulty is in Dale's defence. After a lively opening by the Hatters, Rooney hits an audacious lob shot from within his own half which loops over the Rochdale keeper. Goal of the FA Cup First Round for sure. We will see this classic moment replayed many times. On fourteen minutes Alex Reid slots home after good work by Connor Jennings. A dream start.

Dale improve in the first half forcing County into a more defensive formation. Matty Lund heads in to score for the home team and the Hatters are on the back foot. A strong finish to the first half by County preserves our 2-1 advantage at half time. Excellent work from the boys.

In the second half ex-Dale player Jordan Williams makes his debut coming on for Ryan Croasdale. Rochdale bombard Ben Hinchliffe's goal forcing our keeper into three good saves. It was rear guard action for most of the second half but County produced an excellent defensive display. Coupled with our impressive first twenty-five minutes when we dominated play, Jim Gannon will be well pleased with this solid display against a team two divisions higher.

Sunday 29th November 2020- F A Cup Second Round
County 3 v Yeovil 2 AET

County have had three weeks off due to positive coronavirus tests within the squad. Another crazy turn to the season that finds County slipping down the table to twelfth with other teams racking up games as the Hatters "self-isolate." Seven National League matches are planned for December in a rejigged fixture list. Some schedule, but the squad should be well rested and ready to gain ground on the teams above.

It seems like we've had another pre-season break since Rochdale in round two as we gear up for consecutive cup matches.

County beat Yeovil in the FA Cup 3-1 away two years ago and 5-0 at Edgeley Park in 2008. Hopefully, this is a good omen. The last time we got to the third round was in 2007 going out at Watford. County scored first before losing out 4-1 to the Premier League outfit. Hatters fans were in fine voice that day as we easily filled our allocation. The prize today is to go into the third-round draw with the big boys from the Premier League and Championship. The match is live on BBC digital. In my new virtual viewing reality I will be watching via my trusty laptop. I have seen every minute of every game this season. A couple of matches live in the ground and the rest via the screen.

The news is that as we come out of the second lockdown, limited fans will be allowed into grounds in certain areas. Tier 1 regions are allowed up to 4,000 spectators and tier 2 up to 2,000. Greater Manchester is in tier 3 where no fans are allowed back in yet. Merseyside is tier 2 after their recent testing programme. So my quest to watch every County match goes on in its current virtual reality. Of course, once I am allowed back into live matches, I will be there.

This cup tie could be described as a ding-dong encounter. Or a humdinger of a tussle. After three weeks County football came back with a bang. The Hatters started out the better team before ex-County player Matty Warburton opened the scoring for the Glovers. Matty didn't seem to celebrate which was a nice touch but it was rather predictable that our old favourite would score. Rooney converted a penalty to equalise before Yeovil scored again through a back-post header. Ash Palmer scored a tap in for 2-2 before Yeovil gained a highly dubious penalty. Justice prevailed as Ben Hinchliffe saved.

The game moved into extra time with County on top again and Connor Jennings scored a nice header from a great cross by Jamie Stott. 3-2, good game and into the hat with the big boys for round three. After a rather surreal three week break it was great to get football back. Twelve months ago nobody would believe you if you described this scenario. You would be the conspiracy theorist. Or possibly a member of the flat earth society or just the nutter in the pub. Hopefully, there are no more unscheduled and bizarre interruptions to our campaign.

NB- Monday 30th November. The FA Cup third-round draw is made.

We are drawn against the Hammers of West Ham at home! First thoughts; a League Cup victory over them in the 70's and the Ian Dowie own goal in 96/97. An amazing header that was guided with power perfectly into his own net. The best own goal I've ever seen. The only explanation being that Ian was just trying get rid as powerfully as possible. With no imminent danger he may have got a cheeky shout from one of our players. Or he just thought- I am going to head this for a corner- but then his inner-striker took over and his goal-scorer radar forced the header into his own goal. Great stuff.

CHAPTER TWELVE
December 2020

Saturday 5th December 2020

Bromley 0 v County 2

Back to league action after a month and we are now lying thirteenth in the table. A false position as most teams have played four or five games more. We had the break due to the positive coronavirus test in the squad. County have played FA Cup games though and now find themselves up against Premier League West Ham in the third round. All in all this is shaping up to be a bloody good season. There is a big challenge now to catch up these league games and bag a decent points haul.

Bromley's Hayes Lane will have fans in attendance. No away fans allowed. Bromley find themselves in tier 2 being in South London which means they are allowed up to 2,000 fans in their ground. Shall I risk a cheeky step ladder perch like my Guiseley exploits? Or impersonate a South Londoner and try to pass off as a home fan? I have decided that in the spirit of social consciousness, I will be a good boy and remain in my tier 3 provincial zone. You are not supposed to travel outside your tier 3 area. It would be a shame for a middle-aged County fan to be reprimanded by the law for travelling to watch his team. Strange days indeed.

I am in my now familiar virtual viewing living room location as I tune into the Bromley live stream. The Ravens or the Lillywhite's as they are known are in their fifth year in the National League. County played Bromley for the first-time last season taking a creditable four points, 2-2 away and a 1-0 win at Edgeley Park. Random fact about Bromley is that their record attendance of 11,000 was versus a Nigeria

XI in 1948. The current capacity of Hayes Lane is 5,000. Either the ground was significantly bigger or the crowd was significantly squashed back in '48.

The Hatters enter the arena resplendent in fluorescent yellow. The teams rather natty and lucky third kit. One which I nearly bought recently until I remembered that men of my vintage should not wear modern kits. Maybe a cotton retro non-sponsor version. But the modern nylon with a sponsor adorned across the chest is not the best look at my age. I do look young if I must say so myself but the replica kit should be banned post 40 years of age. Then again, I may be tempted. I digress.

It is a lovely sunny day in Cheshire and the same can be said for South London. So much so that straight after the match I am riding over to a mates on the trusty Royal Enfield. Any dry opportunity at this time of the year must be utilised for motorbiking.

First thing of note is it is great to see fans in the ground. Hayes Lane is decent too. Good sized stand behind one goal, decent covered terrace behind the other and a nice full-length terrace down the side of the pitch. Jennings, Reid and Bennett are on in an attacking line up. Nyal Bell has been loaned out to Halifax to get some games under his belt. One for the future. The pitch is a 4G synthetic surface.

The Ravens make a lively start putting the Hatters on the back foot. Jennings hits the post with a great shot after ten minutes then Hinchliffe makes a great save with his chin. Our keeper gets four minutes of treatment. On fifteen minutes Reid gets a fortuitous goal as the ball ricochets off him from five yards out. Alex proceeds to celebrate in front of the home fans and then gets jeers throughout the first half. The jeers intensify when Reid should have made it 2-0. It is great to have the banter of fans back. On half time Bromley should have scored and the Hatters went into the break with a rather flattering 1-0 advantage.

Minihan came on for Reid at half time and provided a nice low cross that Rooney slotted home on the hour mark.

Bromley were always in this game and it wasn't until the last fifteen minutes that County controlled the play. A good away result and we did look like an organised outfit. The stream was good but the Bromley commentators sounded glad to get off their gantry and into the warmth of the club house at the end.

With a spring in my step I wrapped up, got on the Royal Enfield, rode to my mates and had several celebratory beers. Just in case you wondered I didn't get back on my bike. Life is good and I look forward to Barnet away on Tuesday night.

Tuesday 8th December 2020

Barnet 1 v County 2

Jim Gannon and his men return to the capital for consecutive away matches this time to North London. Just three days earlier we dispatched South Londoners Bromley who were in form. Barnet are out of form and there for the taking. In truth, away matches are never straight forward. Among the County faithful there is an anticipation that we are going to win all our games in hand and catch up the leaders. It is unlikely that we will gain maximum points from the four or five games in hand. Patience is required.

Confidence was further bolstered this week as the club released a video updating supporters on all the improvements taking place at Edgeley Park. In addition to the new cladding of the Cheadle End, refurbished club shop and dugouts there is a lot happening behind the scenes. Brand new dressing rooms, refurbished concourses under the stands and the executive suites are being transformed. The club have left no stone unturned in the quality of the works. The standard is that of the Championship or even Premier League level. The ground itself is still the same capacity but the works are of a very high standard.

Barnet have annoyed me again and I'll tell you why in a minute. I wasn't going to mention their tactics of last season but I will. You may recall that they jumped above us into the play-offs. We were the form team but they had played a few games less due to questionable postponements. The points per game system calculated Barnet would finish above us. The reason for the postponements was that their pitch was waterlogged for three National League games. This was timed around a cup match where it was convenient to rest players. You may say that might be a bit of a scurrilous accusation. However, their pitch is only seven years old so should have all the modern drainage.

Now Barnet have decided to charge £12.95 for their stream of tonight's match. All the streams up to now have been between £7.99 and £9.99 including other London clubs. Only a few quid but nevertheless another annoying Barnet detail. I also don't like their flat pack, leisure centre type ground either. They are still getting my £12.95 though so they have kind of won on that score.

The score of the match is what counts. Our beloved Hatters line-up with two changes as Minihan and Jordan Williams start. Barnet line-up with poet Wordsworth and fashion designer Alexander McQueen. Or their namesakes. The pre-match entertainment includes an interview with the Bees manager Peter Beadle. This is conducted by their media executive who looks about fifteen years old. The young man is then part of their commentary team. The stream is a bit jittery as Barnet gain revenge on my complaining.

The Bees look there for the taking in the opening ten minutes before getting into the game. Bennett and Reid are linking up well with Rooney pulling the strings in midfield. It is with some relief in the forty second minute when Reid scores. A Bennett flick on is controlled and then Alex produces a cool chip over the keeper.

In the second half Barnet continue brightly and equalise with a well taken curling shot past County keeper Hinchliffe. We then should be two up as the unlucky Bennett hits the post. Reid and Bennett have played really-well and are developing a good understanding. Then in the fifty-fifth minute there is poetic justice as Wordsworth is sent off for a two footed challenge on Sam Minihan. On seventy-three minutes another flick on by Bennett finds Reid who converts for what would be the winner.

Two impressive notes to take away from this match. Reid and Bennett are developing into a good strike combo. This is a consecutive away match where County have seen late pressure from the opposition but have played the game out professionally. No panic and sensible game management in the last five minutes. The sign of a team that could win this league.

NB- County have drawn Chorley or Guiseley in the F A Trophy. The Government's tier review is on 16th Dec, so the Chorley/Guiseley tie on the 19th could be the first game back at Edgeley Park for supporters. Fingers crossed.

Also, chuffed to announce that Victor Publishing have decided to publish this book. This is the same publisher that published Phil Brennan's The Man from Uruguay, the excellent biography of Danny Bergara.

Tuesday 15th December 2020

Notts County 1 v County 0

I am involved in the construction industry so at least I can go out to work rather than work from home. I worked all the way through the first and second lockdown and thankfully wasn't furloughed. Football provides an escape for many people. Attending the match in person is key for many fans who use the event as their socialising as well as supporting their team. The live streams have been a good replacement but nothing like the real thing. Especially in the northwest where football is etched into the social fabric of society.

As a teenager living in sunny California, football fanaticism was always there. I played for several teams in the American Youth Soccer Association (AYSO) a national network of youth football. Very organised and the standard was high. Even though I lived four blocks from the beach, some of my most anticipated moments were postal deliveries from my grandparents back in Stockport. Shoot and Match magazines were regularly dispatched from Blighty. There were expat British pubs and shops that sold expat papers which would feature football results sometimes a month old. These would only feature the top English and Scottish divisions.

For any younger readers, I must put some context into this. This is the early to mid-80's. No internet, just snail mail. Unless you dialled a long-distance phone call. As a result, I requested the Stockport Express from the other side of the Atlantic. That way I could read some write ups and get the occasional snapshot of Mickey Quinn scoring for the Hatters. Being a County fan was difficult back in those days. Even if you got hold of a proper British paper sometimes County's result wasn't even there. As we played at home on a Friday night, they seemed to miss the result out like we didn't exist.

Well we do now. This team is on the up and tonight we need to get back on track towards the top of league.

I have visited Meadow Lane on three occasions the first being one of my random matches in the mid-90's. A mid-week game with a Bolton supporting work mate. The Trotters ground out a point if memory serves me right. The other two games were in the early 2000's with the Hatters when we drew on both occasions.

I was a bit disappointed with Meadow Lane. The Magpies are the oldest professional football club in the world. Their black and white stripes inspired Juventus. On that basis I was expecting something characterful or distinguished about their ground. Maybe I am too much of a purist. The stadium is a typically boxy early 90's refurbishment. The architect and club gave the design a rather perfunctory style. In their defence they were probably working to a budget and went with a practical execution.

My disappointment with Meadow Lane was probably influenced by the impressive City Ground, home of Nottingham Forest. Magpies fans won't thank me for that. While Meadow Lane nestles amongst industrial units, the City Ground nestles nicely on the banks of the River Trent.

A neat and tidy stadium with good design to the stands that overlook the water. You can walk behind the ground along the river with the adjacent rowing clubs offering a bit of character. Like Fulham's Craven Cottage.

My only visit to the City Ground was to witness Mark Robin's save Alex Ferguson's job. His goal clinched a third round FA Cup victory in January 1990. Although United's chairman at the time Martin Edwards denies it, Fergie was a dead man walking. Three years of underwhelming football and mid table finishes were wearing thin amongst the United faithful. The club was sliding further and further away from Liverpool and some of the home matches would put an insomniac to sleep. How things changed.

County should be fresh as Saturday's home match against Sutton was postponed at the last minute. En route some of the away teams entourage displayed "flu" like symptoms. Frustratingly the game was called off at 10:30am. Another game to squeeze into the new year.

Good news from my perspective is that it has been announced by the club that all season ticket holders will get into all league matches if we are moved into tier two. Tomorrow the tiers are reviewed and there is a possibility that Greater Manchester will be moved into tier two allowing 2,000 fans into the matches. Apparently circa 500 fans requested a refund meaning that retained season tickets are around 2,000. Season ticket holders get first dibs on cup matches. This guarantees Jonnie and I West Ham tickets.

Onto the game and I'm glad I have done the intro reference the Nottingham grounds as there isn't much to say about this fixture. We huffed and puffed. We had three corners and one shot on target from Rooney as he tried to slot a chance past their keeper. Reid had an angled shot past the post early on. Apart from that, County were sloppy with their passing and nothing came of set pieces. Notts were resolute, scored early and remained solid at the back.

County made a double substitution at half time bringing on Connor Jennings and Adam Thomas. Adam was substituted himself. After being the victim of a late challenge and receiving treatment, he returned to the pitch to claim immediate retribution on the perpetrator. Summarily booked, Jim Gannon pulled him off for Croasdale.

Frustratingly, the Magpies weren't particularly impressive themselves but solid. County normally would have caused them more problems but nobody really performed that well, meaning we have missed the opportunity to catch up with the top of the league. Our remaining three or four games in hand being the only room for positivity tonight.

Tomorrow may bring some good news about the possibility of Greater Manchester moving into tier two so we can attend Saturday's match.

Saturday 19th December 2020- FA Trophy First Round
County 3 v Guiseley 1

The FA Trophy provides a route to Wembley but in this particular season most Hatters fans see this competition as a hindrance. Focus is on the league and our fixtures are getting condensed into the second half of the season. It is likely that the team today will be significantly changed to give first teamers a rest.

My plan to attend matches has become increasingly more frustrating. We play Guiseley today and I hark affectionately back to my blag into their ground in the pre-season friendly. Then on that balmy evening in September it seemed like the pandemic had peaked. The forecast was that we would be back in grounds by October. History has proved that the pandemic would not go away. The idea of blags and press passes and views from outside the ground dissipated as the virus situation became more serious. No clubs were entertaining extra press passes. Just one for the Stockport Express/ Manchester Evening News and our reporter Sam Byrne.

The government decided not to move us back into tier two this week. Even though our infection rates are significantly reduced and some of the lowest in the county. They have moved London and much of the south into tier three. With the impending Xmas break, the government is erring on the side of caution. Shame really as we just received our season tickets as the club anticipated the possibility we may be let in today.

In fact, we received two season tickets each. One for our seats in the Pop side and a temporary one for seats in the Railway End. Until covid restrictions are fully lifted our return to EP will be in our version of the Gene Kelly stand. The roof-less end of the ground where we may be singing in the rain. This is to spread us out for social distancing.

It is great to see another new flag in the Cheadle End. The County California flag from a fellow Stopfordian now living on the west coast of the US. It includes the British flag and the flag of California. Something I am familiar with having lived there for a few years in the 80's. As I mentioned earlier in the book, I got regular updates from Stockport while living in California. I must have received the only copies of the Stockport Express & Advertiser to ever land in LA or the US in general. You never know there might still be part of said paper under the carpet in my old apartment. Probably discovered by an unsuspecting American wondering who the moustachioed soccer player is on the back page. Mickey Quinn of course.

As expected, Jim has made changes. Seven changes from the Notts County match. Barnes is in the nets; Harvey Gilmour is in midfield with Southam-Hales in for Sam Minihan. Bennett drops to the bench replaced by Britton who makes his full debut. The first half is even. Britton heads against the post before the Lions of Guiseley take the lead from a breakaway as Wafula slots the ball under Barnes. Most of the action is in the middle of the field. Not a classic. So much so that I am looking at the Railway End wondering exactly where my temporary season ticket is going to be. There is one block of seats that hasn't been replaced and we are probably in there.

It starts raining in the second half and I contemplate whether the warmth of my living room is preferable to being sat in the roof-less Railway End. I've been out on the Royal Enfield today through Glossop over Holme Moss to Holmfirth and back through Mossley over the tops of the Pennines and Saddleworth. Lovely day until the recent precipitation.

In the fifty-fourth minute Reid is fouled in the box just as he was clean through. Ben Sherriff their number five is sent off for his transgression. The advantage is mitigated as Reid blazes the spot kick over the bar. This brings the Hatters into life as they try to make up for the penalty miss and take advantage of the extra man. The rain is now hammering it down. I'm now thinking of the Walsall fans in the Railway End when we had a tsunami during a match in the early 2000's. I think I am going to get wet in there at some point this season if we are let back in.

We are making hard work of this against ten men. We beat these 5-1 in pre-season when I was the lone County fan in their Nethermoor Park ground. Conditions get worse as County keep pushing for the equaliser and start to look decent. Williams and Rooney come on in the seventy-fifth minute proving that Jim Gannon wants to win this game.

Almost immediately Reid scores a header at the near post from a corner. On eighty-two minutes Reid scores again as he slots the ball inside the right post from six yards. Rooney then scores a peach of a goal on ninety minutes. From just outside the box the shot fades to the top right corner of the net.

Kitching is man of the match and Rooney unsurprisingly made a big difference when he came on. Through to the next round and one more step to Wembley.

Tuesday 22nd December 2020

Hartlepool United 4 v County 0

There is another unfortunate twist in the pandemic. Even though vaccinations have started for the over 80's, a new strain has been discovered forcing the southeast of England into a newly created tier four. No travel over Xmas and the original five-day Xmas bubbles being reduced to just Xmas Day. Plus only your own household allowed in the bubble. Tier three is slightly less onerous. This means that there isn't much chance of a tier review for us until the middle of January. So, it is unlikely that we will be back in EP before then. That unfortunately includes the West Ham FA Cup game. On to our game tonight.

I have been to watch County at Victoria Park a couple of times. Once in the 2000's and once in the late 80's. Both were freezing nights and both ended in draws if memory serves me right. Both weren't classics. That is the reality of lower league football. Away matches were in the main for hard core supporters. If you are not battling for play-offs or in a cup run, teams like County and Pools have spent much of their history in a mid- table vacuum. Sporadic periods such as the 90's and a couple of seasons around 2008 and 2018 being the exception to the rule in our case.

Luckily for us we now have a benefactor that has supplemented our recent National North championship win to produce a massive feel-good factor. You can't say we didn't deserve it after what amounted to fifteen years of decline since around the year 2000. Apart from 2008 of course. 2008 in hindsight was built on borrowed money but now we have foundations of solid rock.

I drove past Victoria Park recently with work and the ground is nicely situated in the town centre with traditional spotlights. Hartlepool has a waterfront and docked there is HMS Trincomalee which is the oldest British warship afloat. The town is better than some may imagine.

I was pretty sure that the club nickname is Pools but it is in fact the Monkey Hangers. I knew the story but I didn't realise they use it. Nothing too sinister in the name really but in this age of political correctness you may have thought it might be an RSPCA issue. The story (or legend) is that the only survivor from a French ship sunk in a storm was a monkey during the Napoleonic War. The locals hanged him as a spy. The club mascot H'Angus the Monkey was elected as mayor of Hartlepool as a publicity stunt in the 2000's. It sounds slightly dodgy now I think about it.

Like Barnet, Wrexham and Chesterfield, The Monkey Hangers have struggled recently. Ex-Football League clubs battling away in mid-table or the lower reaches of the league. That is where we may have been without the takeover. We are in fact currently tenth ourselves but we have three or four games in hand on all the teams above us. If we won all these games, we would be second. However, it is never straight forward as was demonstrated by losing at Notts County in our last game. We didn't play well so tonight is a must win match or at least an opportunity for a much-improved performance.

The first teamers are back in tonight. Up front for Pools is Alun Armstrong's son which makes me feel a bit old. Alun's era at County is unbelievably circa twenty-five years ago. Time flies when you're having fun. Within five minutes of the stream the sound goes a bit Norman Collier. The joys of non-league media production. Keeping the comedy theme going, the two commentators are like the Chuckle Brothers. Pools score on seven minutes. A good breakaway and finish greeted by our commentators with an over-the-top celebration exclaiming the goal by Quaker Oates as they called him. It is in fact Reece Oates.

On sixteen minutes Luke Armstrong goes into a challenge with his head low and Ash Palmer catches him in the face with a high foot. Straight red. Could have been a yellow. Keane drops into defence. The Monkey Hangers don't have many clear-cut chances and are not making the best of their advantage. But within five minutes of the second half Johnson scores to make it 0-2. It may be an own goal by Bennett. Five minutes later Alun Armstrong's son confirms that he is not going to do us any favours by making it three for Pools.

As if it couldn't get any worse, our midfield maestro Rooney gets himself sent off for foul and abusive language to the linesman. Something along the lines of you cheating something. The second word probably starting with a t or a c. Now down to nine men the game is most definitely over.

We did once start a game with nine men against Bury in 1981 and won 1-0. Several of our players lived around Sheffield and car shared. Their journey across to Gigg Lane was delayed. We played the whole first half with the County nine.

That man Armstrong scored a second for him and a fourth for the Monkey Hangers. It finishes 0-4. A bit of a disaster but we didn't give up and finished the game OK putting a shift in with reduced numbers. I predict the hair dryer treatment from Jim for one or two of the lads. No need to panic but that is one of our games in hand wasted. Hartlepool were there for the taking if we kept all our players on the pitch. Next up a local derby away at Alty.

Saturday 26th December 2020

Altrincham 1 v County 1

What I really wanted for Xmas was to be inside Moss Lane to see this local derby. The pandemic keeps pushing attendance back. County need to start shaping themselves for the faithful fans and for the theme of this book. I was confident this log of matches would result in a return to the football league. The Hatters fans are now doubting County's promotion credentials after consecutive league defeats.

Alty are my favourite other team in non-league. I want County to score as many goals as possible today but I do have a soft spot for the Robins. My Granddad moved to Stockport in the 60's but was Altrincham born and bred. Although a staunch Red Devil, he frequented Moss Lane and one of his sisters was a big Alty fan. As kids me and my brother would attend the odd match as the Robins regularly won or did well at the top of the non-league pyramid. They were a big team in the Cheshire League in the 50's and 60's.

They won the top division in non-league four times but were never voted into the league. Twice in the 60's and twice in the 80's. Both times in consecutive seasons.

Particularly unfortunate were their consecutive victories in 1980 and 1981 in what was called the Alliance Premier League. They really should have been elected to the Football League by then. The gentleman's club of Fourth Division directors carried on protecting the clubs seeking re-election. County had to apply for re-election a few times in that era but not in those two seasons. So we didn't directly prevent Alty from election.

I consider myself fortunate to have had the non-league experience at Alty. Moss Lane is one of my favourite grounds. Three sides of terracing and decent size for non-league. Home fans can change ends at half time. If you keep an eye out for the stewards you can still have a cheeky can of beer or cigarette. The top of the Pop side is the best place for that. Quite refreshing for a Premier League fan if you take them there for the first time. The joys of non-league.

Today, all affinity goes out the window as I want the County boys to stuff the Robins. Alty are on a better run of form over the last five league matches but we have beat them in all our four league meetings. I attended our two victories at Moss Lane. On this occasion we meet them as they occupy their highest league position since we started playing our Cheshire neighbours. Alty are sixth as we lie thirteenth in the table. But we do have three games in hand and are only two points behind them. That is how closely packed this league is. Two or three wins in a row would catapult you up this table.

The Scarf Bergara Wore podcast has a feature which takes the mickey out of some of our more sceptical supporters. They refer to them as bed-wetters. Every supporter deserves an opinion but in these days of social media they have a platform for knee jerk reactions. As soon as we lose a couple of games, we get the predictable Gannon out brigade. After the Notts County defeat and below par performance there was understandable disappoint as three points would have put us right back at the top. Against Hartlepool we got a red card after fifteen minute and were down to nine men in the second half. We must write those two matches off and get behind the team and manager.

I have watched every minute of every match up until now. If you recall from earlier in the book, I said this would be the most challenging potential "fixture" clash. The big family gathering has been cancelled for today due to covid rules. However, my daughter is coming over and my Mum. We are supplementing yesterday's leftovers with fresh meat and veg but inevitably its timing will be during the Alty match and live stream. However, I think they have decided that since I have been pottering away on this book for over six months, they are happy for me to have the stream playing.

The fallout from the last match versus Hartlepool means that Palmer and Rooney are suspended after their red card indiscretions. I managed to watch the match between being host and pot washer. The first fifteen minutes had technical issues as the Alty stream kept freezing with the on-screen clock frustratingly ticking along. Bennett was on the bench. Plus the loss of the red card offenders meant replacements Jennings, Lois Maynard and Adam Thomas started. We were camped around their box for large parts of the first half before the Robins went 1-0 up through Ceesay as he slotted under Hinchliffe.

Cue gentle ribbing from my lads as they reminded me of my early season prediction that we would smash this league. The only team smashing this league are Torquay. We seemed to be huffing and puffing without many clear-cut chances. This follows the recent trend in our league performances. Overall we were the better side and with ten minutes to go Connor Jennings flicked in at the near post from a corner to score. Decent point. But in the context of it being one point from the last nine, there were many doubters on social media. Most of us Hatters are now having a reality check and focussing on the play-off positions rather than automatic promotion.

In a festive alcohol haze, I am still positive about a title challenge though. With only a third of the season gone and three consecutive home games in the next week, we may have a loftier position by early in the new year.

Monday 28th December 2020

County 2 v Wrexham 0

Yesterday we had a family walk around Rainow in the peak district as a traditional romp in the country to blow the festive cobwebs away. With the dust settled after another under-whelming County performance, the Hatters faithful have undergone their usual analysis of progress on social media. The consensus falls into two camps. The sceptical and the realistic. The sceptical I predict are the younger element and the anti-Gannon brigade.

The realistic are more likely to be the older match going supporters that have seen several decades of ups and downs. Some forget that we had a terrible start to our iconic 96/97 campaign. Or a slow start to our National North championship season. Seasons develop in stages and it is rare that a team stays at the top all year. Although currently, Torquay are having a good go.

The Gulls won again on Boxing Day 6-1 against Yeovil. They have opened a nine-point gap at the top. Fifteen points ahead of County but we have three games in hand. The Hatters have only played twelve league games though which is less than a third of the season. Our team is taking more time than expected to gel but my glass is still half full.

Today we play Wrexham. I am not keen on Wrexham. I am sure they have some lovely supporters. However, on our visits to the Racecourse Ground some of their fans see us as a big club from a neighbouring English county. Fairly local and more importantly English. What should be just two big clubs playing a league match, inevitably includes goading between the Welsh and English. Some of our more excitable element are more than happy to oblige.

Unfortunately, there won't be any supporters in Edgeley Park today as we continue in the covid supporter lockdown. Shame as today would have been one of our biggest crowds of the season. We beat them at their place last August 2-1 with 1,000 County fans roaring us on. The reverse fixture was postponed due to the pandemic. Our visitors are on the same twenty points as County having played one more game.

Wrexham have recently been bought out by Hollywood stars Ryan Reynolds and Rob McElhenney in an unexpected takeover. Supporter-owned, the fans couldn't believe their luck and must have thought it was a Chester FC inspired prank. Chester are their local rivals.

Bennett is back in the team to partner Reid upfront with Rooney and Palmer still suspended. The first half is excellent and the best we have played since Rochdale in the FA Cup. Post Rochdale we have had a couple of solid away wins in the league and an FA Trophy victory against Guiseley. Decent but not convincing. The Notts County and Hartlepool defeats were well below par. Even the point at Alty wasn't too impressive. Today, County looked like a proper side in the first half.

On the front foot from the kick-off, the Hatters scored on twelve minutes. Connor Jennings provided a nice flick to Southam-Hales who delivered a good cross along the six-yard box for Bennett to slot home. Within two minutes Jordan Keane scored a great header from a Southam-Hales corner for his first goal of the season. Just before half time Reid hit the bar with a header, Maynard re-directs the rebound but Wrexham clear off their goal line. Some great one touch passing on display. Southam-Hales is having a stormer.

Shame that the fans aren't in to cheer the lads on. I reckon there would over 6,000 in Edgeley Park today under normal circumstances.

Wrexham manager Dean Keates must have thrown a few teacups around the dressing room at half time as the Red

Dragons come out with more of roar. Re-energised, our visitors should have scored through Ponticelli. He fluffed his lines in front of goal. His name reminded me of the 1970's American TV series about a legal investigator called Petrocelli.

County had another couple of chances to put the game to bed. Bennett and Reid could have scored with Connor Jennings providing some great through balls. Wrexham had one deflected shot that looped on to our bar. The Welshmen's last throw of the dice was to put on Yussuf up front to no avail. County commentator Jon Keighren informed us that the Wrexham sub was once banned for five games after having a pee behind the stand during a warm-up when a Mansfield player. Sounds harsh.

We are up to fourth in the table after a much-improved performance. Leaders Torquay dropped points with a draw at Weymouth but they will take some catching up. Plenty of time though.

CHAPTER THIRTEEN
January 2021

Saturday 2nd January 2021

County 2 v Altrincham 2

This is the traditional festive season return match. A tradition that continues in non-league when we play a local rival within a week home and away. A tradition all leagues did back in the day. The First Division even joined in up until the 1960's. This was to help the supporters with local derbies during the holiday period. Also to help the players get home more easily. There was a time when matches were played on Xmas Day!

After the uplifting performance in our last match against Wrexham, we are all feeling more optimistic. Xmas has brought us good tidings. The year 2020 has turned out very well for Stockport County. In general though, it has been a bit of an annus horribilis with the pandemic. But for County we have returned to the National League and done well before the season was curtailed early in March. In January it was confirmed that Mark Stott and his Vita Group had taken over the club. A County fan with genuine financial investment. Since then the development of the team and refurbishment of the stadium has been undertaken professionally and smoothly.

Since March, under difficult circumstances, several new players have arrived and integrated well into the now fully professional squad. There have been some below par displays but overall we have done well. The team sits fourth in the league and we are still in both cup competitions with the West Ham game to look forward to.

It is unlikely that fans will be in the grounds before Easter if at all this season. The country is almost entirely in Tier 4 now and pretty much in lockdown to try to stem the tide of the new variant of the virus. Good news is that a new UK manufactured vaccine has been OKd to supplement the first vaccine. With the season less than a third complete I still hold out hope that we will return to Edgeley Park this season. It will be June before the fixtures are concluded.

Today, the man in charge, Jim Gannon undertakes his 500th game as manager of Stockport County. Over three spells with two promotions often under severe financial restrictions. Jim also played 480 times over ten years scoring an impressive 64 goals from midfield or defence. Jim was nicknamed the Ghost as he would often appear in great positions surprising the opposition defenders and scoring for the Hatters. County Hall of Famer Jim could be described as a living legend.

The line-up sees Rooney return after suspension replacing Connor Jennings who drops out due to injury. The rest of the team is the same as the Wrexham victory. It is brass monkey's out there with the temperature just above freezing. The Railway End seats look decidedly Baltic. That is where I should be in my socially distanced temporary seat. The only upside of not being there is that my living room is nicely climate controlled. The centre circle advertising canvass is rolled away exposing a circle of green turf. The rest of the pitch is speckled in white frost and fresh snow.

County dominate the opening stages playing slick football. On five minutes a superb finish by Reid from a Southam-Hales cross at the near post, puts the Hatters in front. County have another one disallowed after Croasdale converts from an offside position. Alty come into the game towards the end of the first half with Cissey who scored against us on Boxing day looking lively. Cissey plays for our opponents based near Baguley but was born in Barcelona. The weather is more Baltic than Barca with heavy snow beginning to fall.

At half time, the first half scoring combination of Reid and Southam-Hales are subbed presumably with knocks and replaced by Williams and Thomas. On fifty-five minutes Rooney puts County 2-0 ahead with another sublime goal that curls into the top right-hand corner of the net. However, Alty are playing well. Their manager Phil Parkinson makes some good substitutions with Hancock in particular having an impact. On seventy minutes that man Cissey slots home for the Robins.

The visitors are now in the ascendancy in what is an excellent end to end game. Within five minutes Colclough scores past an unsighted Hinchliffe and the match is level. Alty have matched us in the second half and with a couple of minutes left Peers forces Hinchliffe into a fine save.

Our enforced substitutions had an impact on our second half performance but credit to Alty for making it a great game. Fortunately, Torquay lost away at Yeovil to at least keep their gap down somewhat at the top. On this display, Alty and ourselves should finish near the top of league and hopefully in the play-off positions. Catching Torquay looks like a tall order as we remain in fourth position.

Monday 11th January 2021 – F A Cup Third Round
County 0 v West Ham 1

The TV cameras return to Edgeley Park for national coverage. BT are here with both teams covid tested on Saturday and ready to go. David Moyes announced last week that West Ham will have a strong line-up of first teamers with one or two changes. Just how it should be for the biggest cup competition in world football. We are at full strength with Palmer back after suspension.

The whole country is in a new lockdown until mid- February to try to stem the tide of the virus and provide a mass vaccination of the elderly and vulnerable. Good job we have plenty of football to watch.

This is a massive game for County. Probably our biggest game since we played Carlisle in 2006 and just stayed in the football league in front of 10,000 fans. Our National North champions game at Nuneaton was probably the biggest achievement-wise since the Carlisle game. Along with our 2008 play-off win. Our refurbished Edgeley Park will look great on telly. It is like fate has brought us Mark Stott to refurbish the ground and squad for this moment as the main match on TV. This is the only cup tie on tonight and with the nation in lockdown this will be one of the largest TV audiences ever for a County match. The match is worth £100,000 to the club.

We also got a main feature spot on Football Focus on Saturday. In typical fashion when a lower league club achieves such coverage, the content was hit and miss. It started with a visit to our new training ground and interview with Jim Gannon. Jim explained how he joined in 1990, bought a house in Edgeley, married a local girl and became a County legend. Also, about being a West Ham fan as a kid through his Granddad when he spent some of his childhood in London.

Then, co-host Mark Lawrenson rather amusingly proved that he does little preparation for his appearances on TV. First-off he wondered what a virtual ticket was. Marine have sold nearly 30,000 for their cup tie against Spurs. Then he thought he had played against Jim Gannon which he hasn't. Certainly not in a league or cup match. He was probably thinking of when County played at Anfield in 1984. At the time Jim was a mere 16-year-old lad who wouldn't make his Dundalk debut for three years. Then, Lawro said that when the Hatters were in the football league our ground was the nearest ground to the Mersey. It still is. Plus I don't think anyone has moved the River Mersey.

Lawro presumably drives over to the Salford Quays studio, grabs a coffee, some free buffet, has a bit of banter with the crew, sits down and just says anything that comes to mind. Not bad work if you can get it.

As with matches of this magnitude it is good to check our historical record against the opposition. We have played the Hammers seven times at EP going back to when we were both in the Second Division in the 1920's. In seven games at Edgeley Park we have never lost. In fact we have won six and drawn one. Amazing. That includes two 2-1 League Cup victories. The well-known 1996 victory with the Ian Dowie own goal. Also, the 1972 League Cup victory against a West Ham side including Bobby Moore, Billy Bonds and Trevor Brooking. Our overall record versus our visitors is an impressive won 7 drawn 3 lost 4. Of course we are now further away from each other than at any point in history. Tonight would be a major upset. In fact it would be a non-league team beating a Premier league team.

I have been selling this game to the family for weeks. The missus has even started asking when are County playing West Ham? The lads even watched the Football Focus feature twice just for the novelty of seeing County on national telly. Jonnie has his white County away shirt ready. It is almost like preparing for a Cup Final. This is the magic of the FA Cup, sometimes lost on Premier league fans or younger generation fans. At one time as I have mentioned before, winning the FA Cup was as big as winning the First Division. Certainly when I was a kid growing up in the 1970's. County won't win the Cup. But the thrill of this match after years of struggle is a big buzz for Hatters fans.

The coverage starts at 7pm for an 8pm kick off. This year is unique as the fourth and fifth round draws will be held before the match. This is something to do with allowing teams plenty of preparation time for future fixtures in case covid interferes with plans. County will know their potential opponents for the next two rounds if we should be victorious this evening. Of course my heart says a victory. This would provide one of the biggest "giant killings" of modern times. While my mind suggests more caution with the fact that there are five divisions between us and the Hammers . Oh well, I am determined to enjoy this match. It could be anything from a 2-1 victory to a 0-5 defeat. I need to be realistic but come on you Hatters!

This morning two doors down had County scarves hanging out of the bedroom windows. That will be Harry who is

County mad. Our similar aged son Jonnie has his County shirt on and I've just got one day of work until the big kick off later on. I hung a County scarf out of the window too. I'm sure the missus will enter into the spirit of the day.

The conditions can only be described as biblical as the rain descends on Edgeley Park all afternoon and all the way through the match. A platform has been erected in the corner between the Cheadle End and Barlow Stand providing a perch for co-presenter Paul Scholes. Paul's dulcet tones laud County as a big club with a great old-fashioned ground and loyal support. In the studio Peter Crouch assists in the fourth and fifth round draws. County or West Ham get Doncaster and the winner of that tie would play Liverpool or Man United. We start to dream of an upset tonight.

The Hatters line up at full strength albeit with Palmer on the bench and a flat back four as a tactical switch from our usual 5-3-2. County start brightly but the Hammers are dominating midfield with Rice and Noble showing their Premier League pedigree. The fake background noise disappointingly doesn't include any Edgeley Park standards such as The Scarf my Father Wore. Instead we get what sounds like a steady stream of shouting kids. On fifteen minutes the match is temporarily stopped as five minutes of loud fireworks go off behind the Railway End. It is presumed to be County fans but they are a tribute to a local lad who got knocked down recently and is in a bad condition in hospital.

We hold our own through-out the match in torrid conditions. There is one patch in the corner below Scholesy which is particularly pond-like. Kitching gains advantage for County by kicking it into this patch and running on to the ball which has been held up in the sodden turf. Croasdale and Maynard are playing their socks off in defensive midfield while captain Hogan is having a storming match at the back. The lads are playing really well with the exception of some disappointing set pieces.

It looks like extra time until one lapse of concentration results in a goal for the visitors. In the eighty- second minute

Rochdale lad Dawson is unmarked and heads in from a deep cross. Jim makes a few substitutions including a rare sighting of academy player Hinchy who came on for Rooney.

A brave performance by the boys. Some disappointment. On reflection a bit of relief too. If we had played extra time in those conditions and then had the distraction of a potential match with Liverpool or United, it could have affected our focus on the league. Great coverage for the club and excellent experience for the players. The night was a success. Now back to our bread and butter.

Saturday 16th January 2021 FA Trophy Second Round
County 1 v Notts County 2

This match provides an opportunity to make amends for our under-performance a month ago at Meadow Lane. In that away fixture v Notts County, the lads missed a chance to capitalise on games in hand in the league. Notts are by no means pushovers but in that match the Magpies did not perform well and we were average resulting in a 0-1 defeat. That defeat was followed by victory over Guiseley in the FA Trophy but then our worst performance of the season losing 0-4 at Hartlepool in the league. This provided a blip in our league form and set a few alarm bells ringing.

Fortunately, we have been much improved since. It seems like Jim Gannon has steadied the ship and the psychological development of the team. He is a disciplinarian and has a way of playing. This squad now seems tuned into Jim's frequency.

We return to cup action again today in the FA Trophy. Out of the FA Cup, the Hatters still have a chance of a trip to Wembley in this competition. I think the FA Cup would have been a big distraction. However, if we concentrate on the league and take the Trophy seriously that might be a good idea. Promotion is the priority but it would be amazing to do the double of promotion and a Wembley cup win. Or why not the ultimate double of champions and cup winners! Aim high boys.

History bodes well as the Magpies haven't won a competitive game at Edgeley Park since 1965 – a run of nine games without a victory. Today is the first anniversary of the takeover of Mark Stott. Ground improvements continue with scaffolding erected at the Railway End. There will be a new scoreboard installed. The pitch is in playable condition despite the deluge on Monday night.

The County line-up sees seven changes reflected by a similar number in the Notts team. Both teams have long trips on Tuesday with us at Dagenham and the Magpies travelling to Yeovil.

Josh Barnes is in the nets with Thomas, Southam-Hales, Bennett and James Jennings also coming in. County enter the field in our florescent third kit as a tribute to Khia Whitehead. Khia is a promising young local footballer who was recently knocked down and suffered life changing injuries.

In the opening minutes both teams look lively and serious about this competition which County lost in the semi-finals to Fylde a couple of years ago.

The first half develops without any clear-cut chances until the half hour mark when teenager Jimmy Knowles tucks away a chance from near the penalty spot to give Notts the lead. On thirty-six minutes Southam-Hales delivers a perfect corner that causes panic in the box before Ash Palmer taps in at the back post for the equaliser.

In the second half Thomas hits the post, Bennett should have scored and both teams make subs to try to win the game before the match goes straight to penalties after ninety minutes. County shade the second half before Notts seal the win with an eighty-eighth minute deflected goal. Scorer Kyle Wootton hits it from outside the box and the unlucky Jamie Stott deflected past the helpless Josh Barnes.

The Hatters drop out of two cups in one week. We played OK but I don't think there will be many disappointed County fans. The league is the main feast and Dagenham are next on the menu on Tuesday.

Tuesday 19th January 2021

Dagenham & Redbridge 0 v County 2

We are down in East London to play the Daggers. With work over the years, I spent a fair bit of time in these parts and I am familiar with the drive down the A13, the main artery into East London from the M25. Dagenham is known for its massive Ford car plants and the acres of council estates that housed the workers from the 1930's onwards. The rather uninterestingly named Chigwell Construction Stadium is blocked in between houses and industrial estates of mainly building supply outlets. It is possibly the drabbest location of any ground I have visited. Sorry Daggers fans.

The club were only formed in 1992 as an amalgamation of Dagenham and Redbridge Forest. They quickly navigated themselves through the Conference to League Two and even spent one year in League One. Brilliant effort for a club that has probably reached that height with the lowest ever average attendance for that level. No surprise for an amalgamation club that have West Ham, Orient and Spurs nearby. My visit watching County ended in a 1-1 draw.

Unsurprisingly the stadium is about right for the National League rather than the Football league. One decent stand behind a goal, a hotch-potch of seating down both sides and just a wall behind the other goal. Redbridge moved into Dagenham's home which opened in 1917 and is known as Victoria Rd to fans. A repeat 1-1 draw tonight would be a big disappointment as we need to really push on in the league now. The Daggers lie at the bottom end of the table and have struggled to score goals. If we have aspirations of automatic promotion, we need three points.

Debate since our double cup knockouts this week has turned to the requirement to some-how usurp Torquay at the top of the league. The Gulls are well ahead at the moment. Even if we win our three games in-hand we would still be two points behind. Not unassailable but still a challenge. Especially if Torquay continue their consistent form. My theory is that there are two areas for improvement. Bennett, Bell or someone needs to supplement Reid's goals up front. Or we buy a striker. If not, then our set pieces need to improve dramatically to create more goals from the likes of Palmer and Hogan with headers from corners or free kicks.

Our general play has been good but set pieces have been disappointing. We have had the most shots in the league. Fortunately, our midfield with Rooney etc has chipped in with the goals. We have a high corner count but a low percentage of goals from set pieces. Something to work on.

Hopefully, we will see this season out. News yesterday emerged that the next tranche of Covid-19 cash from the government will be a loan rather than a grant. The government gave the National Leagues £10M in the first half of the season as a grant from the lottery fund. The second funding figure of £11M will now be loans rather than grants. So it will need to be paid back, something most clubs won't be able to do as the vast majority don't turn a profit. Dover are furloughing players and threatening to drop out of their fixtures.

Fingers crossed something will be sorted. I don't fancy the idea of null and voiding this book after fifty odd thousand words! Oh well, I'll keep going until someone tells me it has all been cancelled. Always look on the bright side of life.

Tonight, I will be staying at home of course and watching on the Daggers pay per view live stream at £9.99. Some fans have decided to forgo the cost in case the season is cancelled. Apparently, there is a meeting tomorrow between the National League and the clubs. The National League's track record has been distinctly non-league in previous negotiations and communication with the government from what I have heard. Hopefully, everyone gets their act together so I can finish this book.

It is back to our recognised starting line-up as the Hatters jog purposefully onto the pitch resplendent in the all-white away kit. Entering from the tunnel positioned in the middle of the big stand behind the goal where the County faithful would normally be gathered. County start in a high tempo fashion. The Daggers commentators are decent. The older fella is a decent geezer and one of their goalkeeping coaches. His younger cohort sounds OK but pronounces our players as Scott, Crossdale and Hinchcliffe. He later corrects Scott to Stott.

Our corners are much better as per my request earlier and my theories for areas of improvement. Maynard plays well in a first half of few chances with Reid going the closest to scoring. After the break we begin to dominate and on fifty minutes Bennett tucks home a rebound off the keeper from a shot rifled in by Rooney. Reid is unlucky again as he blocks a clearance by their keeper but the ricochet goes just wide. Alex gets third time lucky on sixty-seven minutes. Well, there is no luck as he skilfully controls a long pass before slotting home inside the post. Great skill by Reid.

The last fifteen minutes are expertly marshalled by County as Bennett remains a loan striker after Reid is subbed. The back line were immense tonight. Rooney, Croasdale and Maynard put on a controlled midfield display and the two front men both scored. Not the best first half but overall a perfect away performance. Three points in the bag, back on the coach up to Cheshire and Boreham Wood at home on Saturday.

Saturday 23rd January 2021

County 1 v Boreham Wood 1

In a season that couldn't possibly get more bizarre it just took another surprising twist. On Thursday after nigh on 1000 matches as player and manager, Jim Gannon was sacked. In his third spell as manager, County are joint third in the table. The decision was met with almost unanimous consternation within our fan base. Jim is a legend of the club. There were rumours before Christmas that a few key players had fallen out with or complained about Jim. Maybe this was a factor. But you would think there must be more to it. The board issued a short statement explaining that the decision was not results based but is centred around culture.

Assistant Manager Dave Conlon will take interim charge whilst a new manager is appointed.

The question over whether the league will be concluded still lingers. On Thursday it was confirmed that the National League North & South has been suspended for two weeks as they consider the implications of the government grants becoming loans. Both those leagues have a majority of teams voting to void the season. In our National League the majority want to continue. Then yesterday the National League announced that we are on our own in our negotiations with the government body managing the loans. This was the National League outing themselves as a toothless and ineffective organisation. Now there is doubt about the survival of our season. What a season to write a book! Nevertheless, tomorrows match is on.

Earlier in the book I mentioned Boreham Wood when I watched their play-off match with Halifax back in July. If you read that bit and got this far, thank you very much! I hope you have enjoyed this dedication to SCFC. But to recap quickly our opponents are nicknamed The Wood, they play at a tidy re-developed ground called Meadow Park and are located between Barnet and Watford. If I were a Barca fan I would be talking about Madrid, Malaga and San Sebastian. You are presumably a County fan or a lower league aficionado, so we get somewhere between Barnet and Watford. I wouldn't change it for one minute.

Off the back of Tuesdays solid away victory at Dagenham & Redbridge, even the most sceptical Hatters fans were starting to get on board the County promotion express. Belief was that this squad is well drilled, in tune with Jim Gannon and has the magic formula of closing games out and securing the points. Except that Jim has now gone. All the players in hindsight were not on Jim's frequency. So we now have to reset and hope for the best.

The Wood are in good form. In their sixth year in the National League they did the double over us last season. Our commentator Jon Keighren made a heartfelt tribute to

Jim Gannon. Also a mention for John Jeffers our ex-player who tragically passed away recently. Jon also informed us that a new manager will be in place for next Saturday's game at Woking.

With snow still on the pitch from this morning's storm an orange ball would be useful but for some reason we don't have one. When the ball goes out for throw-ins it gets lost in the piles of snow. Fortunately, we are now implementing spare balls on cones strategically placed around the pitch. On six minutes County make a perfect start when Rooney curls a free kick from the side of the box into the top corner of the net. The Woods rather bulky keeper resplendent in tight fitting pink kit is left stranded and looking a bit ridiculous. Five minutes later our keeper Hinchliffe makes an amazing save thwarting a deflection from three yards.

Ben Hinchliffe makes three more great saves as Boreham Wood are the better side for most of the first half. After the break, Hinchliffe made a rare mistake letting a shot in at his near post as our opponents equalise on the hour. Bennett made a great run before a last-ditch block. From the resulting corner Reid hits the bar from a near post glancing header. That's about it from us.

The Wood are a physically imposing side and well drilled. Their back line and midfield are all big lads and they played a solid line across the park which County struggled to penetrate. The pitch cut up and was sticky sapping the energy out of us by the last ten minutes. I was glad of the point by the end.

Saturday 30th January 2021

Woking 1 v County 4

Our new manager is 39-year-old Simon Rusk. Who, you may ask? The same question asked by 100% of our fan base. He was a highly rated under-23's coach at Brighton. Not filling you full of confidence. Me neither. Sounds like a master plan involving our Director of Football Simon

Wilson. He himself being a young football analyst. For a fan of my vintage it all sounds a bit risky.

There has been a massive amount of reaction on social media to Jim's sacking and the predicted induction of Mr Risk. Sorry, Rusk. Probably more than Frank Lampard who also got sacked this week. Frank of course was at the mercy of a Russian oligarch. I am fully behind Mr Stott and his investment. I am still undecided about our new structure with Simon Wilson football "analyst" as Director of Football. In a modern trend we have this position as someone who identifies new players and drives the club culture.

In theory a young well qualified and highly recommended coach is a good fit for this structure. Fair enough but we are County and we are trying to get out of non-league. Wrexham have been in this league for 12 years. It is not easy to escape and usually happens with the guidance of an experienced manager at this level. I still think Jim was a better bet to get us out of this league and then maybe we could change the model. Fingers crossed I am wrong and Simon Rusk is the man to get us promoted.

Mr Rusk is joined by veteran ex-player and manager Mark McGhee as his assistant. Dave Conlon is retained and forms a threesome as first team coach. Good to see Dave retained and this provides a good bridge for the squad into the new set up.

I've never been to Woking for a match but have scouted around the ground on my work travels. It is a typical non-league stadium with one big stand behind a goal which dwarves the other sides. The Cardinals gained promotion to the National Conference in the mid 90's and have stayed there since with the exception of the odd short spell in the Conference South. Lying southwest of London the County coach will rack up excess miles on another long-distance sortie. There is a case for changing to regional divisions and splitting this league into North & South. This would require some re-jigging of the current Conference North and South.

However, there is benefit in having lower travel costs and more local derbies generating larger crowds.

To the game itself, this was one of the best performances of the season. The first half was impressive with County going in at half time 3-0 up. Second half was a professional display as the Cards came back into proceedings. The perfect start on two minutes saw Connor Jennings slot home at the back post. Rooney added to his impressive array of conversions this season with a nicely side-footed goal from eighteen yards. On half time Southam-Hales slotted home from another great cross by Kitching.

Diarra pulled one back early in the second half before Reid netted a nice left foot drive across the keeper. We even had a cheeky County fan ask the Woking commentary team to make a dedication for Arthur Brownlow's "99th birthday". A promising debut by our new management team. Even for a big Jim Gannon fan like myself, I have to say this was a great start for Simon Rusk and this performance bodes well for the future.

CHAPTER FOURTEEN
February 2021

Tuesday 2nd February 2021

County 0 v Sutton United 2

Think of Sutton and I automatically recall a cracking giant killing in 1989. Coventry were defeated 2-1 in the third round of the FA Cup by our visitors. Coventry had been winners over Spurs in the final in '87 in an exciting 3-2 victory for the sky blues. Epitomised by the classic stooping header and winning goal from Coventry's Keith Houchen in extra-time. Sutton overcame their First Division opposition from the West Midlands at their characterful Gander Green Lane.

Sutton are a team with triple nicknames. Affectionately known as The Us, Ambers or Chocolates and Yellows amongst their brethren. We played them twice last year and both matches ended 0-0 so it is time for some goals in this fixture. Sutton have been in this league for a few years while we worked our way out of the tier below. It is still a shock to recall how far County fell but there is light at the end of the tunnel now.

As a football nut I was caught watching a pre-match documentary. You could call it an hors d'oeuvre before the main football feast at Edgeley Park. The topic is something that my 19 and 16-year-old lads can relate to from my youth. The programme; Stuck on You: The Football Sticker Story. About four Italian brothers called Panini who took a childhood obsession into a worldwide multi-billion-pound industry. Kath has now officially given up on curtailing my footy urges!

This match was a victim of another covid scare last December and has been re-arranged for today. Sutton reported members of their entourage as having "flu" like symptoms and the match was frustratingly postponed at 10:30am on the day of the match.

Returning to the refurbished New Edgeley Park as I refer to it now, we are looking for home advantage to steer us to three points. When I say New Edgeley Park I may as well treat you to one of my motorbiking analogies. It is like when you love an old classic bike but it is a bit dated and knackered. Spruce up the engine and polish up the fairings. Four wheels move the body, two wheels move the soul. EP is a classic old school ground and we are lucky to have her. These flat pack stadium don't move the soul.

Talking about the soul, unfortunately today will be another virtual experience. I am attending in spirit rather than the freedom of my season ticket seat. A sense of "freedom" akin to the visceral emotion of riding a motorbike rather than being trapped in a tin can (car). I have watched every minute of every match of this campaign. Pre-season matches at Colne and Guiseley were the only games I attended in the ground. The rest have been viewed by streams. Great coverage but trapped in the four walls of my living room. Like being in a car rather than feeling the freedom on a motorbike.

Enough of the amateur psychology, what about the match? Well before the game, another quick motorbike story. After installing a new battery that cost me a fortune, as the choice wasn't great under lockdown, I had another breakdown. The battery itself is fine, it even works down to minus 18 degrees Celsius (just in case I fancy an excursion to Siberia). Seeing as only essential travel is allowed, that is unlikely.

Yesterday as I was riding along, the bike cut out near the Strawberry Gardens pub in Offerton. Something to do with fuel (no, I didn't run out.) I checked all the fuel lines and breather hoses. With limited tools and patience, I pushed it for a bit before I could freewheel all the way downhill. Past the market to a bike shop in the town centre and left it there.

Hopefully, Sutton don't have similar problems and actually get to EP this time.

This match is a classic six pointer. The Us have the same points as us, having played the same number of games with the same goal difference. We are third courtesy of alphabetical order. Sutton have lost two of the last five while we are unbeaten in the last five in the league. Simon Rusk had a great start on Saturday when we dismantled Woking 4-1. Woking were poor in the first half when we racked up a 3-0 advantage. Nevertheless, it was a great performance and bodes well.

Unfortunately, this was a basket case of a match. County came out at 100mph. Then Hinchliffe let a back pass under his foot for an own goal and we lost our impetus. Hogan gave away a pen but actually got the ball and got sent off. An appeal will be submitted. We had bad luck and the players became frustrated. A few of our players lost their discipline.

Our visitors are a big physical unit and once they got their noses ahead, they closed us down every time we got near their box. Against ten men Sutton got solid banks of players behind the ball and played out a perfect away performance.

Was Woking just a lucky 4-1 against a poor team? Rusk needs time and a performance against Yeovil. Sutton was just one of those games to put behind us.

Saturday 6th February 2021

County 1 v Yeovil 0

Back on live BT telly against our West Country opponents, County really need three points today. We have dropped to fifth but have games in hand as Sutton and Alty leapfrogged us on Tuesday night. Fortunately, Torquay were defeated by Altrincham at home to keep the gap down. If we could go on a run and win two or three of our games in hand, we could be in striking distance of the Gulls. It is all ifs and buts and up until now we have failed to capitalise on Torquay's slip ups.

There was a touch of indiscipline in the ranks as we scrambled around the pitch with ten men against Sutton. Something Rusk needs to work on. Composure is the key word for me at the moment. We have the players, but they seem in a rush to win matches rather than complete a calm and organised performance. This team still hasn't fully gelled. There have been signs but now is the time for Rusk to set his style into the performances. To be fair, this is only his third match but such is the anticipation within the County fanbase the pressure is on for a proper run of consistent performances.

We move forward with Animo Et Fide - with courage and faith. That's what it says on the Stockport coat of arms and our old badge. The new circular badge doesn't have the motto included but it sounds good anyway. Seriously though, we do need this faith today. We have a new signing in the ranks. Will Collar is a holding midfielder signed from Hamilton of the Scottish Premier and an ex- academy player under Simon Rusk at Brighton.

Collar didn't play. Simon Rusk said it was a bit early since signing but will be part of the action in forthcoming weeks. The match kicked off with a lady referee at the helm. Very good too- probably one of the best refs I've seen in our non-league days. We started well and another victory over the Glovers similar to our FA Cup second round victory would be perfect. Reid opened the scoring after controlling a clearance from Hinchliffe then slotting calmly home. Another nice conversion by Alex.

Yeovil rarely threatened preferring a strong-arm containment policy. Presumably with the plan of sneaking a goal and being satisfied with an away point. County played well in patches but huffed and puffed in places. Ultimately the single goal delivered the points for the Hatters. A much needed three points to keep us in the promotion hunt.

The main talking point involved Yeovil's strong-arm policy as demonstrated by their chief clogger and captain Collins. In the last minutes of the match Collins launched himself at the ever-impressive Southam-Hales as he broke away to run down the clock. Collins lumbered across and jumped knee high at Southam-Hales when the ball had already been pushed forward completely wiping our man out. The clearest red card I have ever seen. The "challenge" is a shoe in for those Sunday League foul compilations on You Tube.

Saturday 13th February 2021

County 0 v Aldershot Town 0

With a rare full week of training our boys should be well rested and tactically up to date for today's match with "phoenix" club Aldershot. We unusually had Tuesday off allowing Simon Rusk useful time on the training pitch. Tuesday would have been versus Macc but they went bust in the summer. Today we play The Shots. Aldershot FC became the first Football League team to fold during the season since Accrington Stanley in 1962. From the ashes came phoenix club Aldershot Town, who were formed on April 22nd 1992. A situation we probably came very close to over the last twenty years. In fact that situation could easily have occurred in the 70's and 80's too. Our new ownership provides some relief and much optimism for the future.

The Shots are your archetypal lower league club. Perennial members of Division 4. Then extinction before rising through non-league and spending a few years in League 2. Then dropping back into the National League. Their highest ever league position was 8th in Division 3 in 1973/74. This season our visitors are mid-table losing three and winning three of their last six matches.

We re-signed Tom Walker this week on loan to the end of the season from Harrogate. This will be his third spell with County. A popular move with the fans, Tom is straight into the side offering a creative spark. Will Collar is on the bench for the first time. Credit goes to the ground staff for getting the game on in freezing weather with many matches across the country being postponed.

Following the theme in recent games we dominated without creating clear cut chances. County huffed and puffed in the first half in what can only be described as turgid fair. At the start of the second half Bennett missed a sitter from less than a yard. An easy chance, the only excuse is that there was a bobble but it looked like a terrible miss. As Richie only scores occasionally, the miss provided ammunition for his doubters. One bright spot was the introduction of Collar who looked good on the ball. Our misery was compounded when Rooney missed a penalty near the end.

Without a striker on the bench Reid was surprisingly subbed off leaving the shot shy Bennett up front. The mystery is where Nyal Bell has been since his return from Halifax on loan. He seems to have disappeared.

Ifs and buts again with the penalty miss and Bennett's failure to convert a sitter. Apart from that, we still didn't look convincing leaving a very disappointed feeling amongst the County supporters. The Hatters now have two long distance away trips next week with the pressure on to get at least four points. Sutton won again today and lie second in the table two points ahead of us with a game in hand.

Tuesday 16th February 2021
Maidenhead United 0 v County 0

Think of Maidenhead and most people would struggle to pinpoint it on a map. It sounds like it may be coastal but that is Minehead. It is in fact in Berkshire between West London and Reading. County fans have become experts on the towns of England and Wales. Seeing as we have been up and down five divisions over the last twenty years, Hatters supporters must have visited more places than any other set of fans. Founded in 1870 United are one of the oldest clubs in the country. Nicknamed the Magpies, you guessed it, they play in black and white. Tonight Maidenhead celebrate their 150th birthday. Unfortunately there won't be any fans in the ground.

Our opponents are tenth in the table compared to our fourth. They have two games in hand and would leapfrog us by winning both. That is how tight the league is. We are at the half-way stage in our fixtures so there are plenty of points to play for. Our main problem is that we fail to convert our chances. We must have the biggest corner count in the league and up there with attempts on goal. The debate since Saturday between fans is the need for a goal scoring striker to supplement Reid. Either get one in or change the tactics. Or bring back Nyal Bell (wherever he is).

News over the weekend is that Dover have decided to furlough themselves. They claim not to be able to carry on financially if the government grants become loans. They are second from bottom having only completed 15 fixtures. The league could become a 22-team division after Macc went out of business and Dover now preparing to furlough. They are effectively going on strike to force the arm of the government. That is unlikely to happen so their fixtures and results could become null and void. The majority of National League teams do want to carry on. With the likelihood of the National League North & South being cancelled Dover would not be relegated.

Proceedings did not bode well as it was impossible to get on their stream. After multiple attempts I sent a message and they sent me a link. I just made it for kick-off. Maidenhead apologised via twitter with a free link. So I could have saved ten quid. Which would have been welcome as the game itself certainly wasn't worth that amount. Similar to Aldershot, we huffed and puffed. Plenty of possession and neat tippy-tappy football without any end product. In fact, the only shot of note was a great volley by Rooney near the end. The Magpies were big and physical. We need a plan B against these teams. No Nyal Bell in the squad again. We are short of options up front and the way we are playing this limits goal scoring opportunities.

County remain fourth with this point away from home which is OK but entertainment was at a premium. Along the back of the opposite stand to the camera position runs a busy train line which provided almost as much entertainment as the match. You have to question why all these trains are running in lockdown?

Let's hope for better fair on Saturday with another tough awayday at Eastleigh.

Saturday 20th February 2021

Eastleigh 1 v County 0

Our opponents were only formed in 1946. Residing near Southampton, the club started to climb up the pyramid in the early 2000's. They progressed from the Wessex League through the National Conference South and promotion to the National League in 2014. They passed us on their way up. As a result our return back to the National League last year provided our one and only meeting; a 2-0 victory at Edgeley Park. The return match wasn't played due to the suspension of last season.

The club were without an official nickname until 2005 when a competition was run amongst fans and "Spitfires" was chosen. The Spitfire aeroplane was built in Southampton and first flown from Eastleigh Aerodrome, now Southampton Airport. After the club gained its official nickname, the club had an irregular mascot, Sammy the Spitfire, who was a dog. However, in 2015 a new mascot was selected, Brooksy the Bear, in honour of Mr Derik Brooks, who founded the club in 1946. All a bit non-league. I like non-league but a return to play in the football league is long overdue for us.

We need to shape ourselves today and improve our performances if we have designs on getting out of this league. To be fair to Rusk it is early days as he tries to get the team scoring again. Early signs are that he has adopted a play it out from the back philosophy. Then a possession game involving neat triangular passing. Against the big physical teams, a plan B needs to be implemented at some point. At this rate we are going to steadily accrue points in low scoring games and finish just in the play-offs. Then encounter one of these physical teams again in the play-offs and get out muscled.

Hopefully, I will be proved wrong as we go on an impressive run starting today. The pitch looks worse than ours as County enter the Silverlake Stadium in their fluorescent yellow third kit. Down each side there is a sandy strip but as managers often say- it is the same for both sides. We have injuries and suspensions forcing a few changes. Harvey Gilmour starts and new loan signing Sam Dalby is on the bench.

We start well with Will Collar looking impressive again. After being pleasantly surprised with the stream price - £7.99, it freezes for ten minutes. We don't miss much according to their commentator. Then our recent bad luck strikes again. On thirty minutes Gilmour is sent off for what looked like a two footed challenge. Harvey had looked lively and had to wait for his chance in the team. After just half an hour he now has a suspension. Unfortunate as the challenge looked a border line red and probably more of a yellow card.

Down to ten men, we still created more chances and had better possession. The lads put a good shift in but the closest we got was hitting the bar from a looping shot by Rooney near the end. We conceded a soft penalty when Ash Palmer handled from a corner. County had a couple of good shouts for penalties. One bright spot was the introduction of striker Sam Dalby who looked decent.

So, we drop to sixth but the effort was there today and I couldn't complain too much. Rusk is having bad luck with injuries, suspensions, red cards and missed goal scoring opportunities. We are going to have to be patient and hope our luck changes.

Tuesday February 23rd 2021

County 0 v Notts County 0

The Magpies arrive at Edgeley Park in form winning four of their last five games and occupying fifth place. They are just above us on thirty-six points but they have two games in hand. Notts did lose at home to Chesterfield on Saturday and hopefully they will lose again today. We are desperate for three points having hit bad luck and bad results culminating in the 1-0 defeat in our last match preceded by two 0-0 draws. Harvey Gilmour's red card has been rescinded from Saturday which although welcome provided more frustration. If we could have kept eleven men on the pitch, we looked good for three points.

The National League North & South have voted to null and void their season. This has freed up a pool of players to take on loan. We need strikers and we have just bagged two. Chorley duo Elliot Newby and Harry Cardwell have joined until the end of the season. We now have a large squad as the two new recruits supplement recent loan signings Sam Dalby and Tom Walker plus free transfer Will Collar. New recruits are needed with a congested fixture list and heavy pitches resulting in several injuries.

Brilliant news is that we will be back in Edgeley Park this season! Or if everything goes to plan. From May 17th stadiums can allow fans in up to 25% of capacity. Initially the statement talks about larger stadiums but this is promising for us. This means I may be in the ground for the last home match v Woking on the 22nd May. Which would be great for this book. I started the idea almost a year ago planning to attend all matches this season. We know what happened as progressively the pandemic pushed back the ambition of getting in football grounds for this campaign.

With a new spring in my step I feel as if a new start is happening against Notts tonight. Surely our luck must change. Refereeing decisions must even themselves out over the season. We've had more than our fair share of dodgy refs and decisions recently. County will surely start to convert some of their chances and catch-up teams in the table.

In drizzly conditions the Hatters line up with Croasdale, Walker, Gilmour and Dalby starting. Rusk has introduced a more youthful blend in recent matches. Partly due to injuries but there is an indication that the new management team have made their minds up about one or two players and are looking for a younger more technical style.

I can only describe this match as another dose of bad luck. We played well with some outstanding performances but yet again the officials robbed us of three points. This time the unlucky Gilmour was ruled offside after a perfectly good goal. On twenty-eight minutes a quality build up by County saw Harvey convert. With the ref unsighted the liner made the decision. Later, after a check at various angles it was proven to be a perfectly good goal. No VAR at our level of course.

In a tight match involving two solid defences, that one disallowed goal was going to be the difference. Seven hours now without a goal and three 0-0 draws and a 1-0 defeat in the last four games. However, we could have had another six or seven points out of those matches. In addition to the disallowed goal tonight we had other great chances. Reid made a lung bursting fifty-yard break with only the keeper to beat and should have scored. On the hour we were denied by a double goal-line clearance and Rooney nearly scored direct from a corner.

No need to panic as amazingly we are only at the half-way stage of the season at the end of February. The two Chorley loanees should be ready for Saturday to provide further fire power options. Dalby had a good match upfront tonight along with Croasdale, Jennings and Gilmour. I like the look of the new recruits and Gilmour looks impressive now he is in the team. Let's keep the faith.

Saturday February 27th 2021
County 2 v Chesterfield 0

Last match of February and County are just past the half-way stage in the season. As we only started in October the fixtures are condensed into a Saturday- Tuesday- Saturday schedule. Resulting in an end of season finish away at Yeovil on the 29th May. Or hopefully longer if we make the play-offs. At the end of a tumultuous season I may even be reporting on a play-off final! Or even more amazing would be to have a great second half to the season and win the league.

This will be the fourth match of the season versus the Spireites. We lost on pens in the FA Cup but then won the re-arranged match 4-0 after Chesterfield included an ineligible player in the first game. Earlier in the season we won 2-1 at Chesterfield in the league with a late Alex Reid goal taking us to the top of the table. We now lie in sixth with our opponents in mid-table but they are in form having won three and drawn two of their last five. No easy games in this league.

There are eight changes in the Spireites line-up since the last time we played them in November. James Rowe replaced John Pemberton as manager soon after that match and since then thirteen players have been brought in. Results have improved and Chesterfield are one of the form teams. Tom Denton is injured which is a relief. The tall and experienced forward has been a handful in our previous games.

The first half was completely forgettable. It took half an hour until the first shot of the match courtesy of Chesterfield who were playing an un-ambitious style. Clearly looking to frustrate us and hope for a breakaway goal. County lacked urgency and any decent service to Reid and Dalby upfront. Fortunately, Rusk must have provided a good half time team talk.

County dominated the second half and looked a different team. More urgency, more crosses, more service to the forwards and more entertainment. With good pressure building up on the Spireites defence, we made the break-through on the hour mark. Rooney provided a quality chip into the box finding James Jennings perfectly. J J controlled nicely with his left foot before sliding the ball into the net. We got a touch of fortune. In the build up a throw-in was awarded to County when it looked like a Chesterfield throw. With all the bad luck we've had recently it was about time we started to get our share of fortune.

Soon after Dalby was replaced by new loanee Cardwell who held the ball up better. On eighty minutes Reid converted for 2-0 with a nice left foot finish from a similar spot to the first goal. Rusk made a few subs to close the game down with Keane and Collar coming on for Rooney and Walker.

Ryan Croasdale was man of the match and is becoming Mr Consistent in the defensive midfield position. The win took us to third until the late kick-off saw Hartlepool beat Barnet to leapfrog County.

CHAPTER FIFTEEN
March 2021

Saturday March 6th 2021

Weymouth 1 v County 0

Way back at the end of October County lost 2-1 against Weymouth at home. We dominated the first half going in at half-time a goal to the good. In the second half Weymouth scored two break-away goals while we missed good chances. Three points dropped for sure and today we can make up for that defeat against a team currently languishing in the bottom three. We are hoping for a luckier month than February. County had a goal drought last month and some dodgy refereeing decisions that reduced our points haul.

In the home game report, I mentioned I was hoping to make the 260-mile trip to Weymouth on the south coast. March seemed like a long way off and it wasn't until December that events took a turn for the worse and we entered a New Year lockdown. Things are now looking positive for a return for the last home match of the season but until then the virtual match reporting continues. Located down in deepest Dorset, Weymouth is your archetypal seaside town. Known for a white horse etched out of the chalk in a hillside as a tribute to George III completed in 1808. The football club was founded in 1890.

The players warm up on the pitch at the Bob Lucas Stadium. Or the Wessex Stadium as it was known on its official opening in 1987 by Ron Greenwood. Who is Bob Lucas? An ex-player, club president and physio for some 1750 games. Who is Ron Greenwood? Maybe some younger readers may need to know. A decent player for Chelsea, Fulham and Brentford, West Ham manager for thirteen years during one of their most successful periods and England manager for five years from 1977-1982. Interestingly he was born in Burnley but grew up in Wembley. Lucky escape for the young Ron.

In a rather non-league type display the commentators start by holding a paper copy of the team sheet in front of the camera. Then the teams appear with County in our fluorescent yellow shirts. The Terras were nicknamed after the colour of their shirts as in terracotta. At some point they changed to their now familiar claret and blue. Dalby, Collar and Newby are on with Rooney and Southam-Hales joining Kitching on the injured list.

County start the game quickly, controlling the play. This lasts for three minutes before Weymouth break away down the left and convert neatly to take the lead. The Terras look good on the counter similar to the second half at Edgeley Park. Reid has a couple of half chances in the first twenty minutes with Elliott Newby looking good on the ball. Most of our play is going down the left-hand side involving Walker who impresses albeit with not much end product. A frustrating first half ends without County threatening the Weymouth goal.

New boy Cardwell replaces Dalby for the second half. The play follows a similar pattern to the first half with County dominating possession and looking tidy on the ball. At least we go close on a few occasions. Notably a great save on fifty-four minutes, one that shaves the post and two goal line clearances. In the last twenty minutes we get increasingly desperate for a goal. Keane and Bennett come on, we go 3-5-2 and then three up front. The score remains the same with Weymouth doing the double over us. A bottom three side doing the double is not a great omen.

Another frustrating performance. We have seen all the new players and various combinations of squad members since Rusk took over. County have had some bad luck but overall, for all our neat passing, we lack a cutting edge and real penetration when we get near the oppositions box. Food for thought for Rusk. Fortunately, we remain in fourth but we need to string wins together if we want to stay in the play-off positions. Fortunately, I will not spend the next five or six hours travelling back. I can simply walk to the fridge and get a consolation beer.

Tuesday March 9th 2021

Solihull Moors 0 v County 5

The Hatters visit the South Brummies. The residents of Solihull prefer to be associated with Warwickshire but they still have a Birmingham post code. That side of Birmingham is bluenose country as in Birmingham City. Maybe Birmingham's decades of under achievement has resulted in Solihull wanting independence and to try their luck with Solihull Moors. Moors are in fact a fairly recent amalgamation of Moor Green and Solihull Borough. As recent as 2007. Dagenham & Redbridge are another amalgamation team which makes me think that we've had enough years in non-league now. We need to get back to worrying about Oldham and Rochdale or even the likes of Sunderland and Portsmouth etc.

There is still a lot of work to be done before we escape this division though. We started the season on a wave of optimism and joint favourites to be champions. Since then we have flattered to deceive. On one hand we look an organised and well drilled side. On the other hand we don't convert enough chances and are nowhere near clinical enough. Frustratingly, run away leaders Torquay have faded since January and the league is there for the taking for any of the top six. Sutton are on the best run. We just have to hope that our run starts soon.

Our best run was probably last time we met Moors at home early in the season. County sat top of the table after four wins in the opening five games before drawing 0-0 against tonight's opponents. One of those wins was against Dover. Three points that are likely to be expunged if as expected Dover fail to complete their fixtures. The loss of those three points would currently see us drop to seventh. The edge of the play-off zone. The defeat in the opening match against Torquay was followed by four victories. We were the better side against the current table toppers on the opening day and The Hatters faithful were confident of a title challenge. Some even got really excited and considered us runaway favourites to win the league.

Tonight we sit seven points behind the top three. One of those teams, Sutton, have two games in hand and Notts County in sixth have three games in hand and are only two points behind. It is looking increasingly like we are going to struggle to stay in the play-offs never mind battle for top spot. I am not sure how we got into this situation but changing manager hasn't helped. The lack of goals has been a big problem recently.

The two attacking loanees from Chorley have this week been supplemented by another two attacking loanees. Eighteen-year-old Jack Stretton comes in from Derby and twenty-year-old Nathan Shaw from Blackpool. We just have to hope goals come from somewhere.

Injuries have been another recent issue with star man Kitching out for several weeks and our talisman Rooney out for the last match. The impressive Southam-Hales has been injured plus the improving Connor Jennings. It really has been an extremely frustrating period. However, I keep optimistic by convincing myself that each match will be the start of a great run. It is getting critical now but not yet a crisis. Is it a crisis if we don't go up or get in the play-offs? Well, it would be very disappointing. I just can't help thinking that with our squad the league was there for the taking or at least a top three spot. I hope the players realise that although we have plenty of games left, we really do need to get our act together pronto.

The Hatters are resplendent in all white while Moors have ex County players Jamie Ward, Jimmy Ball and 2007/08 promotion hero Stephen Gleeson in their ranks. The boys do indeed answer my wish and get into scoring mode pronto.

With a little help from a Moors defender who trips Cardwell in the box for a penalty and a red card after sixteen minutes. Reliable Rooney converts the spot kick. With numerical advantage County soon put Solihull to the sword.

On nineteen minutes Rooney gets a second by curling a shot nicely inside the post from just outside the box. On twenty-three Cardwell completes a nice breakaway with a right foot shot that bounces off the keeper into the net. On twenty-seven minutes a cross from Minihan is nodded home by Walker. 4-0 at half time.

Of course, four goals in one half changes the mood of recent results, gives the goal difference a boost and pushes us in the right direction towards the top three. In the second half Moors got everyone behind the ball in a self-preservation exercise to keep the score down. County patiently probed. Newby came on for Rooney and new boy Stretton replaced Caldwell who had done well. On seventy-nine minutes Jack Stretton bagged a debut goal tapping in from close range. Job done and a great victory.

With two winnable home games coming up, this might be the run we've been waiting for. Other results were favourable apart from another victory for Sutton who now top the table. On tonight's evidence an assault on the top two looks possible. However, Sutton are now seven points ahead of us with two games in hand. They are due a mixed run so in theory County could make ground on them in the coming weeks.

Tuesday March 16th 2021

County 2 v Barnet 1

Bottom of the league Barnet arrive in SK3. Saturday's match with Dagenham was postponed due to a positive covid test in their camp. We beat the Daggers quite comfortably back in January in what was Jim Gannon's last game in charge. The club at the time gave a brief statement which was unsatisfactory to the fan base. County are used to fan engagement and in Jim we had a leader who gave detailed and honest interviews. Sometimes probably too honest but never-the-less regular and detailed updates. The new regime are cut from a different cloth. Modern, younger and more politically correct shall we say.

The club had been desultory in their communications. They may not have realised. But considering fans haven't been in the ground we were entitled to more updates. With time on my hands due to covid I even developed a Mickey taking old school type fanzine for a few issues. I took the Mickey out of the new regime in a parody of who I thought they may be. It is a fans prerogative to do that. All in good humour of course. Key victim was Simon Wilson our Director of Football.

Credit where credit is due, this week the club released a half hour update from Simon safely managed by our own Jon Keighren as interviewer. This is planned to be a monthly update. Much needed and hats off to them. The content of the interview still contained splatterings of corporate hubris but overall I was impressed. My fake interview in one of the fanzines with Simon still stands as funny (if I should say so myself). But seriously, Simon came across well and I look forward to further updates.

Barnet are now on their third manager of the season. The early curtailment of last season resulted in redundancies at The Hive as the club struggled financially. A poor start to the season led to manager Peter Beadle being replaced by ex-County and England keeper Tim Flowers. Tim left Barnet last week by mutual consent after losing eleven of his twelve games in charge. Unfortunately for Tim and us. I say unfortunate as teams tend to have a bounce back with a new manager. Hopefully, the trend of results under Tim continues and we bag three points. Ex-manager Paul Fairclough takes temporary charge of The Bees.

News overnight is that County have made another John Rooney like signing. Another statement of intent. Fleetwood striker Paddy Madden joins us on a three-year contract for a fee of £250,000. Dropping two divisions, Paddy must have been impressed by our ambitions (as well as the contract). The highly sort after 31-year-old has been a prolific scorer through-out his career. A great signing for us.

Rooney is out injured replaced by Newby. Cardwell starts with new signing Madden on the bench. My pre-match concerns of a Barnet bounce back come to fruition as The Bees provide tough opposition. A lively start to the match resulted in chances for both sides. The best opportunity being a superb glancing header form Cardwell which hit the post from an excellent cross by Newby. On eight minutes The Hatters go ahead. A brilliant cross by Tom Walker is headed by Hogan. The keeper makes a great save before Hogan bundled home the rebound.

Cardwell unfortunately goes off injured after playing well again. New boy Madden comes on and should have scored on the hour. Newby provided another quality cross which Madden heads into the ground from close range. The ball somehow bounces over the bar. Within a minute Minihan has a stinging shot blocked on the line. Two minutes later McQueen scores for Barnet after some great control in the box before pushing the ball past Hinchliffe.

With time running out it looked like we were going to be frustrated after being the better team. Not for the first time this season. Croasdale should have scored towards the end and then substitute Stretton scores for us on eighty-two minutes. A driving run by Minihan resulted in Stretton dinking the ball over the keeper form close range. Fair play to Barnet, they pressurised us to the end.

An invaluable three points with our away game against leaders Sutton approaching on Saturday. They won again tonight in a relentless run since the turn of the year and are ten points ahead of us. If we win, we are only seven points behind. Lose and it is a probably an unassailable thirteen points.

There has been good progress in the last two matches. New recruits are playing well. In particular Newby who was man of the match tonight. Cardwell and Stretton have been impressive. The old guard of Hinchliffe, Minihan and Hogan have been excellent. Croasdale has been consistent. Kitching, Southam-Hales and Rooney will return from injury soon. Madden should be prolific. A top three finish is possible and hopefully Sutton will blow up and let us in to top spot.

Saturday March 20th 2021

Sutton United 1 v County 1

This is the biggest match of the season so far in the league. West Ham was pretty big in the FA Cup. Sutton beat us at home 2-0 on the 2nd February. That day we were both on the same points having played the same games with the same goal difference. Since then Sutton have won seven and drawn one establishing a ten-point gap on The Hatters with a game in hand. By-passing early season pace setters Torquay on the way.

Difficult to gauge our last encounter with the U's. Hogan was sent off after conceding a penalty which was harsh and Hinchliffe let a back pass under his foot for an own goal. One key attribute they have is power which is important in this league. Their team is strong, tough and well drilled with pace in attack. Back in February they went two up and shut up shop forming an impenetrable bank of players. Being down to ten men didn't help. If we could somehow clinch a victory today the gap is down to seven points. That gives us a chance. If not, we would need Sutton to suddenly go off form or pick up key injuries.

Being a seasoned County fan I am better off expecting no points today and anything else is a bonus. Being a half glass full kind of guy I am known for over enthusiasm at times but today is probably a day for calm. Up until about 1990 I literally didn't expect any success for my beloved Hatters. Then a decade of progress/ unbelievable success ensued. Followed by two decades of mainly disaster. With the odd bright spot. Now, Mr Stott has boosted the coffers.

We were on an upward trajectory anyway albeit from the sixth tier of English football. Pre-investment it looked like we would establish ourselves in the National League with the possibility of a promotion campaign in the next few years. Now the plan is multiple promotions in the next few years. Exciting stuff.

Today is a defining moment in our season. The management team will say it is just another game worth up to three points. The fans know it is a massive six pointer. Bar a miracle, defeat will scupper our chances of being Champions. It is a simple as that. I sense a top three finish but let's see what happens.

The elusive Nyal Bell has been located. He is now at Alty on loan. A good move for Nyal as we now have several forwards to choose from. It is a shame local lad Bell couldn't break into the side. He probably isn't quite good enough for us and our ambitions. The capture of Paddy Madden shows our intent.

Earlier in the book I mentioned Sutton's FA Cup giant killing of Coventry back in the 80's. Gander Green Lane has changed since then. The track around the pitch is still there but the surface is now a 4G and behind both goals has been squared off with small terraces. County run on in all white as the Us jog on in all amber. Paddy Madden starts with the impressive Stretton upfront. The match begins at a hundred miles an hour with both teams looking for the win. As expected, Sutton are physical and used to the extra zip off the 4G pitch.

One of their commentators is confident bordering on cocky and annoyingly persists in calling Croasdale Croasendale. In the first ten minutes we somehow keep a Sutton chance out after a mad scramble in our six-yard box after three consecutive corners. Meanwhile Madden hits the bar with a nice flick header off a Minihan cross. Sutton's physical / dirty style is emphasized when their number nine Bugiel went straight through the back of Maynard. No chance of getting the ball, just going straight through the back of his ankles. Yellow card.

By the end of the first half I decided Sutton were similar to the 1980's version of their neighbours Wimbledon. To be fair to Sutton they had the better of the first half with three good chances which went close.

The intensity continued in the second half in what was a great match fiercely contested by two teams going for the win. Sutton made the break-through on fifty-six minutes with a header beating Hinchliffe. The Us then went into a more defensive mode similar to the Edgeley Park match. On this occasion with eleven men on the pitch (as opposed to the home match), County kept creating openings. Southam-Hales and Tom Walker replaced Newby and Stretton. Then Bennett came on.

We had a couple of decent penalty shouts denied. It looked like we were returning to Cheshire empty handed. Until in the ninety-fifth and last minute of the encounter Jennings headed home from a corner. Somehow, with every County player in the box including keeper Hinchliffe, J J found space to nod the ball home. Mad celebrations ensued. A well-deserved and heroic end to the match.

Sutton will regret their time wasting while we celebrate holding the leaders at home and keeping the door open in our pursuit of top spot at the end of the season. Due to the strange development of the season Sutton now have six out of their next seven matches away from home. This is the result of covid postponements and re-arranged fixtures. Hopefully, the away games with impact on their progress. The play-offs are more likely but with the team spirit we showed today, anything is possible.

Tuesday March 23rd 2021

County 3 v Eastleigh 0

Back at EP against the Spitfires from Eastleigh FC. They're from near Southampton and I filled you in on their nickname etc in the away match blog last month. A match we lost 0-1 after Harvey Gilmour was wrongly sent off after half an hour. We were in a run of bad luck and the middle of a goal drought. Since then luck has evened itself out and we have started to score goals. We are in good form. Tonight County are still missing Rooney, Kitching and Connor Jennings to injury. The impressive loanee Sam Dalby, has returned to Woking.

Plus Maynard is away on international duty with St. Kitts and Nevis. I did look up exactly where it is. The island is part of the Leeward Isles in the West Indies. They speak St. Kitts Creole and I wondered if Lois was fluent in his native tongue.

Alex Reid has been a bit out of sorts recently and drops to the bench. This allows Cardwell an opportunity to form a new front line with Paddy Madden. I like both players and look forward to seeing them in attack. Hogan is injured after a heroic performance in our last match at Sutton which allows Palmer a chance. Ash is a more than capable deputy. The Spitfires submit an attacking team sheet with two wingers and two forwards in their starting line-up.

The Hatters are all over The Spitfires in the first half. We are playing an excellent quick passing game which has our opponents scrambling around trying to get the ball off us. We make the break-through on twenty-two minutes. Great work by Will Collar in midfield resulted in a slide rule pass into the box for Cardwell to push the ball past the keeper. Harry Cardwell is playing really well holding the ball up, laying off to team-mates and getting in the right positions. Madden has a trademark flashing header go just wide and we went into the break ahead. We should have been two or three up.

In the second half Eastleigh improved significantly, playing on the break with ex-Hatter Baggie looking lively upfront. On fifty-three minutes County put the game to bed when Madden pushed the ball to Collar who thumped the ball from twenty yards straight past the keeper. A block buster that the keeper had no chance of stopping. County looked composed and were rewarded for their possession again when substitute Alex Reid netted his fifteenth goal of the season. Top scorer Reid headed in from an excellent in-swinging corner from James Jennings.

One of our best performances of the season. Some of our passing and movement was excellent. Difficult to pick a man of the match. Will Collar was a contender with his block buster goal and overall play. Croasdale continues to be Mr Consistent. The Chorley loanee duo of Newby and Cardwell have been a revelation. Newby has deputised for Rooney really well and Cardwell has looked like a more than capable front man at this level. Madden is working his socks off and the goals will come. Ash Palmer was solid as a rock coming in for Hogan.

The teams above us all won so it was important that we did to keep in contact with them. A six-pointer on Saturday now awaits as we entertain second placed Hartlepool at Edgeley Park.

Saturday March 27th 2021
County 1 v Hartlepool United 1

County welcome the Monkey Hangers. Or Pools as they are also known. The rather un-PC Monkey Hanger moniker is their official nickname as explained in my blog for the away game just before Xmas. We got stuffed 0-4 at Victoria Park. Ash Palmer received a harsh red for a high foot then Rooney got his marching orders for excessive industrial language towards the linesman. Hartlepool have an almost invincible home record helping them to second spot in the league. Away from home our opponents have won six, drawn five, lost four. Decent but not as good as the rest of the top four.

Yesterday the National League confirmed that Dover's results have been expunged. They are fined £40,000 and docked twelve points for next season. Unfortunately, this means that we lose our three points from our victory over Dover while it doesn't affect Notts County's defeat.

Resulting in Notts gaining on us. They lie one place behind us in fifth but are now only one point behind with two games in hand. Meanwhile, we are now nine points behind Pools but with three games in hand.

Statistics aside, this is an even match with both teams confident of bagging the three points. Pools are on a great run. We are too and played some great football the other night against Eastleigh. Home advantage should count with at least a point expected. Three points would put us six points behind the Monkey Hangers with three games in hand. Meaning that if we could continue our good form, we are on course for climbing to a top three spot. Catching Sutton looks like a long shot even with fifteen games left to play.

We gained another goalie this week with Ross Fitzsimons arriving from Boston on a short-term loan. Unofficial reports have suggested our new front man Madden is on an eye watering £3,500 a week three-year contract on top of a £250,000 fee. Unprecedented at our level and clear intent that we are gearing up for a quick return to the Football League. Our man Madden starts again today upfront alongside Reid with Cardwell surprisingly dropping to the bench after another good performance against Eastleigh. Rooney, Kitching and Hogan are still injured. Youngster Nathan Shaw makes a start.

Pools manager and ex-County player Dave Challinor has drilled his team well. They are a solid physical unit with tight passing and good movement. Two well matched sides battled away with only two shots on target shared by County's Reid and Pools Shelton in the first half.

Within two minutes of the start of the second half Hartlepool went ahead with a great header by Holohan from an excellent deep cross by Cass. County struggled to get back into the game for fifteen minutes before tactical changes included the introduction of Southam-Hales and Cardwell who had an immediate impact. Reid was sacrificed for Cardwell. The big target man held the ball up as County went direct to chase the equaliser. With the Hatters in the ascendancy, Minihan was substituted for another forward as Stretton entered the fray.

County were rewarded on seventy-seven minutes as a long throw was flicked on by Cardwell and volleyed home by Paddy Madden. Our new high profile forward converted his first goal for County in style. Madden has impressed so far with his work rate and it was great to see Paddy get on the score sheet. A good point in the end with other results being favourable. Torquay lost again meaning we are only three points behind them on the same games and Sutton only drew away at Halifax.

March ends with County improving. Rusk has made a big impact this month with the aid of his signings being a success. Chorley duo Newby and Cardwell have been excellent. County fans are clamouring for the club to sign those two up. Then Madden's arrival is already a success with his great goal today and his excellent work rate. Even with Rooney, Kitching and Hogan out, there is more than enough depth in this squad to compensate. If Sutton weren't so far ahead, I would be confident of competing for top spot. However, a top three spot is possible allowing us passage straight into the play-off semi-finals.

CHAPTER SIXTEEN
April 2021

Friday April 2nd 2021

Aldershot 1 v County 2

A Good Friday trip to Hampshire beckons for the Hatters. Aldershot is known as the home of the British army. Unfortunately for Shots fans and the County away following, we are all confined to barracks as the fan ban continues. There is light at the end of the tunnel with a planned return for crowds at the end of May. Our form predicts that we will be in the play-off mix. This could mean I get into the last home match and potentially a home play-off match.

Crossing everything, a play-off final trip could even be on the cards. However, it wouldn't be at Wembley. The traditional home of the play-off finals will be booked up by then with European Championship matches. The likely venue could be The Britannia Stadium or Villa Park.

Amazingly, on Good Friday we still have thirteen matches left. Of course, the season only started in October. On April 12th the beer gardens open, you can get a haircut and all the shops open their doors. Happy days. I've had my jab and by May pretty much everyone will be vaccinated. The return of civilisation will be complete with the return of crowds at football matches. Over in Europe the outlook is less promising as a third wave beckons in Germany, Italy and France. We have been ahead with our vaccinations and this should prevent another wave during this football season.

At this point, it is probably a good time to praise the work of our manager Simon Rusk. I hope he doesn't look at social media, as the start of his tenure was greeted with doubters and for each below par performance a deluge of criticism.

Part of this could be attributed to fans not being allowed into grounds creating exaggerated frustration and criticism. Replacing Jim Gannon was never going to be easy. However, Rusk has come through a frustrating period where we had some bad luck and poor finishing in front of goal. The last month or so has seen some excellent performances as we returned to the top of the form table. Rusk's recruits have been a success too.

The Shots stream is twelve quid but at least it's on for the best part of an hour before the match. The team sheet shows Stretton, Cardwell and Madden up front as Rooney returns from injury and is on the bench. Richie Bennett has been loaned out to Hartlepool as he can't get in the squad at the moment due to an abundance of attacking options. I've never been to the Recreation Ground but I wouldn't mind. It's a proper old school stadium with plenty of terracing and old stands but a bogey ground, as we've never won there. The Shots are mid-table, losing three out of the last five matches.

With the Hatters resplendent in bright yellow in the Hampshire sunshine we get underway. The impressive pre-match coverage is spoilt a bit by the low camera angle. I imagine a bloke with a camera is stood on a box. County control proceedings and edge ahead after thirty-six minutes when the ever- impressive Stretton slots under the keeper after a nice through ball from Madden.

The second half progresses in a similar vein and we capitalise when a trademark back post header by Ash Palmer nestles in the back of the net from a corner. Somehow the Shots score in the seventy-third minute when Rees benefits from some slack defending and pushes a side foot cross come shot past Hinchliffe. With only one goal in it, a nervy last fifteen minutes beckons but County immediately go back on the attack and control the game until the ref adds on seven minutes. This sparks Aldershot into life and a backs to the wall series of corners and free kicks are defended. The home team failed to score again as we confirmed a well-deserved 2-1 away victory.

Well played by the boys as we keep pace with other results and gain two points on Sutton who drew away at Boreham Wood. An added bonus is that we have won away at Aldershot for the first time after twenty-seven visits stretching back to the 1950's.

Monday 5th April 2021

County 0 v Bromley 0

We are back at Edgeley Park on the telly courtesy of BT Sports for a 5:30 Easter Monday kick-off. We know the other results which include draws by Sutton and Hartlepool and victories for both Notts County and Torquay. Not a bad set of results if we can bag three points today. The County players wear C J t-shirts for the warm-up in support for Connor Jennings battle with a rare form of cancer. The prognosis is favourable and Connor is in the stands watching.

Stuart Crawford has kindly let me have his scrapbooks cataloguing County campaigns from the 80's and 90's. Stuart is secretary at Cheadle Town and a County fan. Match by match newspaper cuttings include the Tranmere match in 1986 that formed the introduction to this book. Brilliant stuff. Loanee Jack Stretton has been unsurprisingly recalled by Derby. Jack was quality for us and looks like a future Derby first teamer.

Meanwhile, out on loan Richie Bennett scored for Hartlepool to secure a point for Pools today. The less than prolific Bennett converted on his Pools debut to assist their play-off chances. The loaning of one of our players to a promotion rival could be questioned. But loaning out players keeps them match fit in case County need Richie for later in the season.

We rarely play well on TV and today didn't change that habit. In a dour 0-0 encounter The Hatters rarely threatened the Bromley goal. The Ravens have a new manager, Andy Woodman, and clubs with new managers usually get a few results. Andy will be chuffed this evening as his game plan worked well. That plan predictably was to settle for a draw.

Bromley packed the defence, got men behind the ball and frustrated Caldwell and Madden.

A crowd in Edgeley Park would have undoubtedly helped. Most of our team haven't experienced a County crowd. This is obviously affecting us at home where the fans would give that extra push when the team needs it. This is playing against us more than for most teams in the league. Our larger crowds compared to the other teams would have been an asset home and away.

The first half featured only two shots on target, both from Rooney. The second half followed a similar pattern with only two shots, this time from Croasdale. A bright spot was the performance of man of the match Tom Walker. Tom provided several good crosses but Cardwell was thwarted each time by Bromley's robust defence.

Reid was on the bench but didn't come on as Rusk unsurprisingly persisted with big money signing Madden. Paddy put a shift in again without threatening the Bromley goal. Rooney looked off the pace as he builds up fitness after his injury lay off. By the end I was wishing Stretton was still available but his impact at County impressed Derby enough to recall him back to Pride Park.

The match didn't provide any footage for the end of season highlights DVD. Ever the optimist, pre-match I was still confident that we might overhaul Sutton and win this league. Without bagging three points today I have succumbed to the realism that we will be in the play-offs.

Back to the training ground in preparation for the big away match in North Wales.

Saturday 10th April 2021

Wrexham 0 v County 3

We've been here before. Typically County flatter to deceive and this season is no exception. The team have performed well in periods until the opportunity to make ground on top spot presents itself and then we draw or lose matches we should be winning. Today, we visit fellow promotion contenders Wrexham followed by two "winnable" home games against Kings Lynn and Maidenhead. Seven points with a draw today would be a great haul and nine would be the business. We are at the business end of the season but will the team deliver?

Simon Rusk has made progress but today is a game where he could really earn his spurs. We have made statement signings and victory today would be a statement result. The club has given the management team the tools to succeed and it's time to deliver. Other clubs have games in hand and there is no guarantee of a play-off position. If we find ourselves in the play-off zone at the end of the season, every point counts. That extra one or two points could put us in the top three providing a home tie in the play-off semi-finals. A massive advantage compared to finishing fourth to seventh.

The Red Dragons are having an indifferent patch losing their last two matches after a resurgence in form. This either means we are playing them at a good time or they are a dangerous wounded outfit. They will be under severe pressure to get a result and return to the play-off positions. It is likely to be a tight match. Wrexham's fire power has been weakened by injuries to key forwards. Kwame Thomas misses the rest of the season and his replacement Jordan Ponticelli is also injured.

If our 2-0 home victory is an omen we should do well. That was one of our best performances of the season. Since then we have strengthened with the signing of Madden and the positive impact of loanees Newby and Cardwell.

Last time we visited The Racecourse Ground in August 2019, a thousand Hatters fans cheered the lads to a 2-1 victory. The stands will be empty this afternoon so the team will need to urge themselves on to three points. I have made a few visits to watch County at Wrexham and there is always a large and raucous County contingent. Our "twelfth" man would have been a big asset today. One benefit is that I am safe from our Welsh mates by watching at home. I once got caught up in a charge of Welshmen outside the ground. They seemed so glad to see us that they ran at us to presumably greet their English neighbours with a traditional welcome. Being completely innocent and just in the wrong place I legged it dropping my steak and kidney pie which I had to purchase again. Maybe this a Welsh repeat business tactic instigated by the local council.

Wrexham's only fit forward is Dior Angus. Interesting name. A combination of fashion designer and Scottishness. He is in fact an ex-electrician and model from Coventry. However, the Red Dragons announce three new signings at 2pm on the day of the match! Including striker Keanu Marsh-Brown who starts alongside Angus.

Both sets of players warm up in Connor Jennings t-shirts dedicated to C J's battle with cancer. Connor has played for both clubs. The players also wear black arm bands in honour of Prince Philip who passed away yesterday at the age of ninety-nine.

County are in all blue with Caldwell, Reid and Madden upfront. Wrexham start the game well pressurising County who were a bit sloppy with their passing. However, on fourteen minutes, a long ball from Hinchliffe over the top of the opposition defence bounces kindly for Reid who controls nicely before hooking the ball with his toe past their keeper to score. Then Alex receives a curling cross on twenty- five minutes from Walker to convert again at the back post from a Cardwell flick on. County are getting plenty of joy down Wrexham's right-hand side threatening the home team regularly in the first half.

Two goals to the good, we continue to put the thumb screws on our hosts in the second half. We are rewarded in the sixty-ninth minute with another goal. Southam-Hales makes a seventy-yard run against the exposed Wrexham defence before being cynically brought down in the box. Rooney converts the penalty to put the game to bed. The remaining twenty minutes are expertly marshalled by a dominant County display.

A perfect away performance notches three more points on the board. Rusk and co will be well happy with this display. The combination of Cardwell supporting Reid was particularly impressive. Also Madden in a withdrawn roll was effective again linking play in cahoots with Rooney. Walker was dangerous out wide and the defence and midfield managed the game nicely against any of Wrexham's attacks.

This was exactly what I was hoping for. A statement performance. With three very winnable games to follow, County have an opportunity to push on into a top three position in the table. A great afternoons work by the players and management team.

Tuesday 13th April 2021

County 4 v Kings Lynn Town 0

County host the carrot crunchers from East Anglia. Maybe that's a bit disingenuous but Kings Lynn, or Lynn as the locals call it is one of those Bermuda Triangle locations. Somewhere way out east located between Norwich, Peterborough and Cambridge. Hard to get to and probably quite a nice place. But in football parlance a club out in the sticks. More about that in our away match visit in two weeks. Tonight is the home encounter, the first of two winnable home games with Maidenhead to follow on Saturday. Then two winnable away matches versus Boreham Wood and tonight's opponents Kings Lynn. Three or four victories should catapult us into the top three.

The players will be full of confidence after a tremendous display in North Wales on Saturday. County comfortably put promotion candidates Wrexham to the sword. We looked solid, organised and dangerous in attack. A similar performance tonight will result in a victory. Lynn are struggling third from bottom of the table. Only Barnet with their disastrous record and Dover's zero points after dropping out of the season occupy the bottom two spots.

County are on an eight-game unbeaten run and field the same side as Saturday's great away win at Wrexham. The

Linnets have a young side playing with freedom after the threat of relegation has gone with no teams dropping out this year. However, on their bench is fifty-year old back up goalkeeper Paul Bastock. There is still hope for me yet then. Paul is also the assistant manager and world record holder of competitive club appearances with 1,280 to his name across a multitude of clubs.

Kings Lynn have secured back-to-back promotions in the last two years ably managed by ex-Norwich legend Ian Culverhouse. Their owner Stephen Cleeve threatened to do a Dover and drop out of the fixtures this season as they struggled financially under the covid climate. Luckily, they were empty promises from the gangster looking philanthropist. Just as well, as Lynn have looked promising recently with a couple of home wins.

There is a nice big new flag in the Railway End proudly pronouncing Heaton Norris Rovers since 1883. But only until 1890 when we converted to the moniker of Stockport County. The Hatters start the match on the attack for the first ten minutes culminating in a twelfth minute header from Madden that bounces off the bar. Within a minute, Paddy volleys towards goal. The shot is going wide but Reid instinctively diverts the ball with his head and it loops over the Lynn goalie. Great start.

The Linnets recover immediately and spend the rest of the first half on the front foot. Their young side are quick and decent on the ball. County play OK but Lynn are very impressive. In the second half County reverse roles and dominate the early exchanges. The Hatters have several chances from headers. Cardwell could have scored when his impressive mane brushes the ball when he should really have powered it home from one yard out. On the hour, the impressive Southam-Hales drives into the box before being tripped. Rooney waits for the keeper to move but dispatches the penalty too close to the keeper and his trailing foot defies John.

Jennings should have scored with his head from one yard out mirroring Cardwell's earlier effort. Then Rooney makes amends for his penalty miss with another sublime goal. A trademark twenty-five yarder is drilled into the top right-hand corner of the net. Reid and Rooney are both on eighteen goals for the season now. On seventy minutes another perfect corner from James Jennings lands on Madden's head who expertly guides it into the Lynn net for our third goal.

The Linnets have nothing to lose and keep throwing players forward keeping the entertainment going. A perfect second half is completed in the eighty-third minute when Madden gets his second goal. Walker pings a great cross to the far post and Paddy heads across the keeper into the opposite side of the net with aplomb. Another clean sheet and four goals to the good.

To top off a great night, the other results are favourable. Sutton lose at home 1-0 to Torquay and Notts County lose 2-1 at Solihull. We are on a roll and it's going to be fun seeing how far we can go.

Saturday 17th April 2021

County 2 v Maidenhead 2

Life is good at the moment. The vaccine is working (in the UK at least), the pubs are open, I've had a beer in a beer garden and County are on the up! Being a glass half full guy, my optimism dial is going up to eleven (if anyone recognises the Spinal Tap volume analogy). In our house I have been known for super-enthusiasm to the amusement of the kids and missus. I am especially buzzing about the footy at the moment resulting in the following statement. Some may disagree. However, if we continue on our current trajectory many will agree.

Here goes. I think the last two matches have had spells of the best football I've ever seen County play in over forty years of watching them. But the actual statement is – "I think our attacking combination of Reid, Madden, Rooney,

Cardwell, Walker, Southam-Hales is the best front six we've ever had!"

There you go. Bold and out there. This combo have been brilliant recently. Madden and Rooney are deadly. Cardwell is a great front man holding the ball up and flicking the ball on brilliantly. Walker and Southam-Hales have been direct and drive into the box creating mayhem. Madden drops into a number ten spot and grafts for Reid who is prolific in front of goal. Rooney is quality on the ball and scores scorchers.

To put it into context, I remember back to around the Les Bradd/ Stuart Lee era who were a fine partnership. I missed the brilliant Mickey Quinn as I was living in America for a few years. Then we had Colville up front, Angell then Francis came in. Soon a golden era of Francis/Preece etc ensued. We had the great team of 96/97 followed by the successful Megson/ Kilner Championship years. We dropped off again but had other attacking heroes such as La Fondre, Beckett, Dickinson, Elding etc. All complimented by good wingers and creative players. But this current team is shaping up to be the best I've seen.

Today we have another chance to gain on our opponents in the top three. If other results keep going for us there is a slight possibility that a miracle may happen and we close in on top spot. Or at least secure a top three position with the reward of a home play-off semi-final match.

Yesterday, with work I was in Rotherham and checked out the Millers New York stadium. An impressive town centre ground albeit a ridiculously named edifice. Literally across the main road is their old home Millmoor. The floodlights are still standing proudly signalling its traditional location. After a number of years the stadium is intact but left to rot away. I went to Millmoor several times watching County. A scruffy ground hemmed in by a scrap yard and industrial units. There is a narrow road that runs down the side of the ground. Downhill and hemmed in by tall factory walls, it was an ominous dark approach to the away end. I drove down it for nostalgic purposes. It was blocked off so I had to reverse back a couple of hundred yards up the narrow lane.

Is the new ground the real Rotherham United? Probably not. An old man in a retro Millers shirt- the one with the big R and U letters on the front, walked passed. I wondered if he would prefer the old or the new. When County get back into the Football League, I will have a little prayer (even though I am not a churchgoer). I will thank the man above for returning The Hatters back to League Two, intact in their spiritual home and relatively unscathed after a long period of hurt. Several times we could have gone under. We could have succumbed to a nefarious owner who uprooted us to an IKEA style flat pack arena next to B & Q or Home Bargains. Fortunately, somehow, we have come out of the other side relatively unscathed and still in our own "house". As Danny Bergara once said, "we've only got a small house but we've got a bloody big heart."

On to today's game. It's a 12:30 kick off as Prince Philips funeral is at three. A well-drilled Maidenhead held us to a 0-0 draw at their place in February. We've kept a clean sheet in seven out of the last nine home games indicating that we should keep the mid-table Magpie's to a blank score card. Having scored seven ourselves in the last two matches without reply, the odds are well in our favour. Sutton and Hartlepool are away at Alty and Wealdstone while Torquay have a day off.

County start with the same starting line-up and bench as the last game against Kings Lynn. No need to change a winning team. The Magpies line-up in red and black hoops reminiscent of Dennis the Menace. Edgeley Park is bathed in sunshine. We have another new flag. This time located in the main stand and dedicated to Connor Jennings. The opening twenty minutes see County control possession but without the lustre of recent performances.

Maidenhead are no slouches though and score on twenty-five minutes when their big centre-half Parry, latches on to a loose ball in the box and hooks it past Hinchliffe. County seem a bit surprised by this transgression and look a bit shaky. Fortunately, we equalise soon after as Reid slides a ball towards goal from the left and Cardwell guides it past their keeper. It's all square at the break as we expect Rusk to give our lads a bit of a roasting during the break.

Roasting or not, County don't look much different. Southam-Hales is our most effective player but as much as we try, nothing is really coming off. Rusk decides to make a change and replaces Walker with Newby after an hour. Newby has an immediate affect providing more energy in our attacks. The Magpies go ahead again, against the run of play. On seventy-three minutes Orsi drives one past Hinchliffe. Our defence has been rock solid recently but today is a below par performance. Our back line have given the opposition more space to work in than usual.

We come from behind again on seventy-seven minutes when Ash Palmer nodded back to Madden who tucked the ball away from five yards. That was about it. We were a bit unlucky but below par compared to recent matches. Southam-Hales is man of the match.

Two points dropped. Good news is our all singing all dancing new scoreboard will start to be erected next week. I think I'd have preferred two more points today though. My enthusiastic introduction to this match blog was maybe slightly premature. Oh well, you can't win them all.

Saturday 24th April 2021

Boreham Wood 0 v County 3

We have a rare week off with no Tuesday fixture. Time for the team to train and work on tactics for today's game. Time to work out why we had a below par performance against Maidenhead. Hopefully, that was a little blip and we will get back to our impressive recent form. I thought after the weekend that this would be a quiet week and a fairly long wait in the perspective of our busy schedule this season. However, typical of this bizarre season of events and force majeure with the pandemic, the relative calm did not last.

First off, let's get the good out of the way. Elliot Newby has signed on a two-year deal. On loan from Chorley, Elliot has been excellent in the middle of the park. Creative and providing regular assists. His fellow Chorley loanee, Cardwell, would be another welcome addition to the full-time staff. Sign him up Stotty! Later in the week, more good news as joint top goal scorer Alex Reid signs a new two-year deal.

To the bad (and the ugly) this week, how about the six Premier League clubs who sneakily signed a contract to become members of a European Super League. A closed shop of twelve clubs who would compete in a mid-week tournament with no relegation. Signing a ridiculously long twenty-three-year contract. How boring would that become! Presumably to service a global audience of new fans and moving matches around the world to China, India and the U S of A. Without consulting their managers, players, fans, Premier League, FA, UEFA or FIFA! The backlash has been unanimous from fans, other clubs, all the football bodies mentioned and the UK government.

Announced on the Sunday evening, within forty-eight hours all six English teams had dropped out of the "Super League". Fan pressure and the overall consensus of the concepts absurdity won in the end. On the same evening American cop Derek Chauvin was found guilty of the murder of George Floyd. Justice prevailed on both counts.

To reality and real football, The Hatters play The Wood this afternoon. Luckily, I've avoided a fixture clash. As mentioned earlier in the book, watching every minute of every match in a season can be quite a challenge. Fixture clash avoidance preparation is a key factor to completing the task. Due to the unusually dry and sunny April, the missus arranged a BBQ for this afternoon. Kick-off 4pm. Fortunately, this morning, the BBQ kick-off was put back to 5:30pm. Nice one. Record intact to date.

County are in the bright yellow away shirts on a sunny day in South Hertfordshire. Reid drops to the bench replaced by

Will Collar as Rusk changes to a more pragmatic line-up. The Wood are another one of those big physical sides typical of this league. Well drilled. Their manager, Sergeant Major Luke Garrard, barks out orders persistently throughout the opening exchanges. Bordering on gobby he berates the ref at every opportunity.

Not much happens in the first fifteen minutes as the ball pings around midfield until Jennings delivers a peach of a corner over to the back post to Ash Palmer who dispatches a trade-mark header into the net. We owe this lot a defeat after they did the double over us last season. The commentators are not going to win any awards. Nice enough but they are making me sleepy. The match isn't a classic but I am roused from my torpor on half an hour when Rooney produces another moment of magic. Twenty yards out, he releases another dipping drive that eludes the Wood keeper. He's a big lad and clad in the skin-tight all pink attire on display at Edgeley Park in the home fixture. The keeper has no chance and hits the deck after straining himself to reach the Rooney dipper.

Garrard keeps berating his players but they don't seem to notice. Which makes me wonder how much players actually hear the manager when they are focussed on the match. It is probably cathartic for the manager though. 2-0 at half time and another professional away half by County. Not the most entertaining fair but we took our chances well.

Second half is better. We start fast from the get-go and The Wood are improved. You can imagine that both managers half-time team talks were along the lines of we haven't won it yet/ we haven't lost it yet. So, get out there on the front foot etc. That's what both sets of players do. One of the commentators refers to our defence as immense all afternoon. Boreham Wood keep knocking at the door but there is no way through. Reid comes on for Cardwell after an hour keeping both strikers fresh. Reid delivers ten minutes later with a drive from eighteen yards to bag the all-important goal. If Wood score it's 2-1 and game on. Instead it's 3-0 and should be enough.

Our hosts don't throw the towel in and keep going. Probably knowing that Sergeant Major Garrard will be waiting for them in the dressing room at the end of the match. Maynard comes on to shore midfield up. Rusk rotates by bringing on Newby for Rooney. It's nice to have a deep squad. Southam-Hales is probably man of the match with another industrious performance. Although, the whole defence were excellent again. That includes our dependable keeper Hinchliffe.

Another solid away performance. After our draw in the last match and victories for our close rivals elsewhere, it looked like third spot may have been slipping away. However, Torquay above us drew and Halifax below us lost today. Meaning we are only five points behind table topping Torquay having played the same games. There will be more twists and turns to this campaign for sure.

Right, job done, well done County. I'm off to do the BBQ duties with a few celebratory beers.

Tuesday 27th April 2021
Kings Lynn Town 0 v County 4

If you are from our opponents neck of the woods you refer to your town as Lynn. Forget the Kings and if you don't, they look at you funny. Lynn is out on a limb somewhere between Peterborough and Norwich. The kind of place where the locals stop talking when a visitor walks into the pub. The Walks Stadium is a proper old school ground. They have been there since 1879 as King Lynn and now their reformed status as King Lynn Town established in 2010 after the original club went bust. The capacity is a decent 8,200 with a good size main stand and three sides of classic terracing.

As fans are still not allowed in, The Hatters faithful won't be in attendance. It may have provided the only chance County fans ever get to visit the ground. Unless you are at least 108 years old as the only time we've played them was in a 7-2 FA Cup victory in 1912 at this venue. Even Arthur Brownlow couldn't have been there. A visit would have been nice but it is our intention to escape this league this season and avoid a repeat visit to the Walks Stadium.

This is another long distance away game. A slow journey too with no direct motorways. One of those trips I looked at earlier in the book as a pain in the arse journey across Woodhead down through Nottinghamshire and across to Norfolk. One I would be more than willing to make if given the opportunity. However, the live streams have been quite handy in combining total viewing of County matches with the relative ease of appeasing family commitments.

After the last match against Boreham Wood, rather than spend at least three hours travelling back, I merely strolled into the back garden. Via the fridge for a beer and then took my position at the BBQ. While entertaining our guests, the missus reminded me that over twenty years ago in our "courting" days I romantically took her to a Stockport County quiz. It was actually in The Florist pub and I won it (the quiz). Much to the chagrin of fellow Hatters "experts" present. Norman Beverley was the "compère". A lovely chap who unfortunately is no longer with us. I don't think I'd get my better half to a County quiz these days!

Stephen Cleeve the Lynn chairman looks a right rogue. I've spent £12 on the stream and that little circle in the centre of the screen is spinning around showing no signal and it is getting close to kick-off. I can only hope it is intended to start just before kick-off. Most streams have started half an hour or more before the whistle blows. I'm getting a bit nervous. Twelve quid is a bit steep too with most clubs charging a tenner or even 7.99. I think only dodgy Barnet have matched this tariff. It's not like King Lynn can claim London weighting either.

Fortunately at about ten minutes before kick-off the picture appears. No sound, just a camera focussed on two high viz wearing geezers stood near the tunnel. I already feel a bit ripped off. Four minutes before the start, the commentator decides to talk. After all my Mickey taking of their provincial location, I wonder whether they have somehow detected my

IP address and intentionally provided me a sub-standard coverage.

Suddenly, the dulcet tones of Stephen Cleeve appear. He sounds a decent bloke. Don't judge a book by its cover my mother once said. The teams jog on with Lynn in a distinctive kit of all blue with a gold and black sash. While the Hatters are in the crisp all white away strip. We are now big time having stayed overnight in Norfolk. Another sign of our full-time professional status this season. Will Collar is out as he woke up with vertigo! In one of the flattest counties in England. Newby starts instead.

Mr Cleeve proceeds to co-commentate. He is very knowledgeable and his cohort impresses when referring to Stockport as in Cheshire. I like these guys. Spirits are raised even higher when County score after only ten minutes. Madden flicks the ball into the net from a Rooney corner. Five minutes later, Jennings curls a corner into the danger area and the unfortunate Gash bundles the ball past his own keeper. The commentary duo hold us in high praise and mention that they'd wish Croasdale would miss the bus home and stay in Kings Lynn. Ryan isn't the only one, as the whole team are impressive.

Lynn are playing OK but leaving themselves exposed at the back allowing County to easily convert their chances. After thirty-seven minutes Newby delivers a wonderful cross from the corner of the eighteen-yard box to an unmarked Cardwell who nods easily into the net. Just before half time, Harry gets his second and County's fourth when a low cross is weakly parried by the keeper for a simple tap in from five yards. A really soft goal which leaves the commentators and I am sure the Linnets manager frustrated. Lynn are decent on the ball but defensive mishaps have provided a flattering score line to County at half time.

The Linnets started the second half well. Fair play to them, they are not giving up but County soon regain control. After an hour Newby is tripped in the box. It looks a bit soft. Rooney takes the pen and is thwarted again by Richardson.

The Lynn keeper saved a Rooney pen in the match at Edgeley Park. The rest of the half played out even. Lynn went up a gear and we understandably conserved our energy with an away match at Halifax on Saturday.

Another professional away performance. Our matches in April close with County on a high. Third spot is looking a good possibility. If results really went our way there is still a small chance that we could threaten top spot. That would require a combination of almost maximum or maximum points for us and some slip ups by others.

Probably the best away commentary team of the season. Knowledgeable, likeable and fair. Mr Cleeve sounds like a thoroughly likeable gent. I take it all back about Kings Lynn. It seems like a very nice place and football club. Twelve quid well spent.

CHAPTER SEVENTEEN
May 2021

Saturday May 1st 2021
FC Halifax Town 0 v County 1

Big match versus the Shaymen today with Halifax lying one place and six points behind us in fourth place. This is a crunch game and should be a cracker. The last time I went to The Shay was about thirty years ago when we nearly went up on the last day of the season. Around 3,000 County fans descended on the West Yorkshire town. The largest away County following I had ever been in. In fact, the following was bigger than our average home attendances in those days. We won 2-1 but other results prevented automatic promotion. Unfortunately, County lost in the play-offs. It was the start of a glorious period though. This year feels similar.

The only other times I've been in such a large County away following were for our games against Man City at Maine Road. A similar size following of 3,000 away fans attended at the Maine Road matches. The 2-1 victory in 1999 in particular still stands out. That is still the best away atmosphere I have been in. County fans literally sang for ninety minutes. The only other time I've been to The Shay was to see Man United win 3-1 in the League Cup. That was around the same time as the County visit thirty years ago.

I don't think the Hatters have played there since. Somehow, we have avoided each other going up and down the leagues.

During our last match against Kings Lynn, the commentators were talking about how ridiculous it is that fans aren't allowed back in grounds yet. Surely it is now safe to attend an outdoor football event. Even if they allowed only 25 or 50% of capacity to start with, why wait until the end of May? Over 60% of the population have had a vaccination with the most vulnerable already receiving their second jab. Kids have been back at school for weeks and the infection rates are still dropping to a very low level.

Straight after the match on Tuesday night I emailed Halifax with a request for a press pass. Mentioning my book and even offering to help out on the day. Almost immediately I got a response form a very polite Kelly- "Thanks for your email – however we are unable to provide any access for external media to our games under our current Covid restrictions. Good luck with the book, Cheers Kel." A polite and expected response but worth a go.

I checked out The Shay on Google maps. It is cut into the ground on one side. Even with its "dug out of the ground" orientation there are no views to blag of the pitch. One side is hemmed in by trees and the other side may offer a sliver of a view from some car show rooms. Not worth the trip. The unfortunate aspect of behind closed doors matches is that a blag is very difficult. With no fans in, if you got in, you would stand out like a sore thumb. Blagging into a normal match with fans is actually much easier. Once in, you just blend in.

For any younger readers, I do not condone blagging free entry to any event or free rides on trains or other forms of transport. I am a responsible (now) middle aged man with a professional career and family. However, I admire youthful ingenuity and intelligence in unlocking opportunities.

Shame about not being in the ground but the streams do offer complete coverage of all County matches this season. The Google search gave me a virtual tour of the Shay. It is a very impressive stadium for this level. Behind both goals they have now completed large terraces. I love a terrace. Along each side are decent refurbished stands providing a similar 10,400 capacity as Edgeley Park. Between the stands and terraces there is still evidence of the grass banks. The old Shay was a charming but run-down grass bowl with dilapidated stands down the sides. It must have been used for speedway or greyhound racing. Now the ends have been squared off with the new covered terraces.

The Shay featured in the Big Match Revisited this morning. An FA Cup third round tie from January 1980 when Fourth Division Halifax beat First Division Man City 1-0. The Shay is there in all its glory. Grass banks and oval track. Pretty much the same as 1990 when County visited in that last match of the season when we had a chance of automatic promotion. The camera panned onto the City bench. Next to Malcolm Allison was ex-County player Stuart Lee. Some great nostalgia in that show.

All sports social media is on a four-day shut down as a demonstration against trolling and racism towards players. Good idea. Hopefully, it will send a message to the companies that run and manage the likes of twitter and Instagram. I've pretty much come off social media mainly using it for updates on County etc. I was never that active. Given my age, I suppose it's not as important to my social communication. I usually just text or phone people. Young people rarely use their phones for phoning which is a bit strange. They communicate via social media apps. It's almost impossible to regulate twitter accounts and the like. Celebrities and journalists are often as bad as the general public so it really has become an evil of modern society in some respects.

It is a bright day in the borough of Calderdale. Ideal for a large contingent of away fans having a day out. With County on a great run and in contention at the top of league, an away following of 2,000 or more would have been expected. What a great atmosphere there could have been. Or should be.

County enter the field resplendent in the fluorescent yellow third kit to avoid a colour clash with The Shaymen's blue and white. Bennett is back from his loan to Hartlepool and joins Reid on the bench as Rusk continues with Madden and Cardwell upfront. Hogan and Maynard return to their ex-club.

The first half sees the Hatters on top for the opening ten minutes until the play falls into an even pattern of possession by both sides. The football is slick with quality passing movements albeit without too much penetration or clear-cut chances. Both teams look impressive and strong promotion candidates. Without a clear-cut chance between them the break-through eventually comes through Paddy Madden just before half time. A ball is flighted towards the goal, knocked on and after a bounce Madden volleyed in from fifteen yards. A superb finish by our new hero showing his quality and football league pedigree.

The second half followed a similar pattern until the last twenty minutes when Halifax increased their press on the County defence. We contained The Shaymen well as they went for the equaliser. Hinchliffe only had to make one save of note in the sixty-seventh minute as he parried a shot away from close range. Maynard came on to bolster the defensive midfield area and played well. Then Bennett replaced Cardwell for the last ten minutes. A thoroughly professional away victory again proving Rusk's credentials as a well organised coach.

With four straight home games before the final match of the season and the trip to Yeovil, County now have an opportunity to rack up more points in their quest for promotion. The penultimate match should see Hatters fans back at Edgeley Park. That home game versus Woking on the 22nd May is etched into County fans calendars.

Monday May 3rd 2021

County 4 v Wealdstone 0

Quick fire return to action today as it is of course May bank holiday Monday. The Stones provide the opposition in the first of four consecutive home matches before the final game of the season away at Yeovil. Saturday's results meant that the table was un-changed as our top four opponents Torquay, Sutton and Hartlepool also won. Wealdstone have lost their last five matches and lie fourth from bottom. Compared to our four wins and a draw the form guide indicates a home win for us.

Yesterday, all hell broke loose at Old Trafford as anti-Glazer/ESL protesters gathered outside the ground, the team's hotel and on the pitch itself. Sounds like a sympathetic steward left a gate open for a couple of hundred over-enthusiastic "fans" to gain access to the bowels and then the pitch of the famous stadium. Unfortunately for United, Liverpool and City et al, the horse has already well and truly bolted. It started with the inception of the Premier League, the eradication of standing terraces and eventually the wholesale selling of the family jewels to nefarious over-seas owners.

Elite European football is bankrupt. Most clubs have over-extended themselves financially to the tune of billions. Now held ransom to over blown player contracts and corrupt agent fees. Even players family members are negotiating their own fees on top of the agents fees. Totally unregulated inflation exists within the top clubs. The German model of majority fan ownership is a solution. However, getting rid of current owners and finding new buyers looks like a mammoth task for the top English clubs.

Rant over, back to Edgeley Park. It is a typical bank holiday Monday- pissing it down. Precipitation all day. Me and the Mrs have already been to North Wales and back on a scouting mission for a potential future residence. We are big fans of coastal life and have designs on a move in a few years. Cardwell, Madden and Reid are in an attacking line-up with Bennett on the bench.

The weather is becoming stormier as kick off approaches. There has been so much rain I half expected there would be a pitch inspection. The wind and rain reminds me of the "tsunami match" of the early 2000's versus Walsall. The one where the game was stopped for twenty minutes as the advertising boards were reclaimed form the Railway End goalmouth. One of only a few matches my wife has attended.

Will Collar is injured and replaced with Reid, showing our strength in depth and attacking intentions. Despite the weather, the pitch looks in great condition. Testament to our new pitch maintenance team. News is that Mark Kitching is out for the season. Wealdstone line-up in silver shirts that fade into pink shapes with pink socks. Call me old fashioned but it looks crap.

County have the ball in the back of the net after only three minutes when Sam Minihan pokes it into the goal but Reid is just offside. We probe for the first half an hour without any clear-cut opportunities.

The Stones look resilient. In the last third of the first half County start to create chances. Cardwell should have scored with a header forcing their keeper into a great save. Minihan had another chance after great control in the box and shot forcing another decent save. Then Rooney went close with a header. Newby replaced the injured Walker.

The weather is getting worse in the second half with a relentless deluge of rain and wind. It doesn't deter the Hatters as they waste no time making a break-through. Within five minutes of the restart Croasdale side foots into the net after some ping pong in the Wealdstone box.

Within five minutes of the break-through, Reid delivers a scruffy shot from seven yards which a defender deflects onto the post then into the net. Reid celebrated what would have been his twentieth goal of the season. But it will go down as a Philips own goal.

Five minutes before the end, Reid dispatches a left footer from the edge of the box which gets a slight deflection. The keeper loses the flight of the ball and is beaten at his near post. In the last minute, Rooney curls a free kick from twenty yards past the keeper who left a big gap on one side. Both John and Alex are now on twenty goals for the season.

Hartlepool lost at Bromley which means County leapfrog the Monkeyhangers into third place. Torquay won to stay top while Sutton play Notts County tomorrow.

No match on Saturday. We should have been playing Dover who have "furloughed" themselves.

Tuesday May 11th 2021

County 1 v Dagenham & Redbridge 1

Back on Tuesday 19th January we played The Daggers away from home, down in East London and came back with a professional 2-0 victory. It was the end of an era for the club. Our leader Jim Gannon was sacked a few days later. It was his last of approx. 1000 matches as player and manager. An absolute legend. It seems a long time ago now but it is less than four months. A lot has happened since then. New boss Simon Rusk had a tricky start before establishing himself with a superb fourteen match unbeaten run. We are the form team in the league.

Last Tuesday I watched Notts County v Sutton live on BT. A great match with Notts taking the lead before being pegged back to 2-2 then winning the match through a penalty in injury time at the end. This result kept us one point behind Sutton in third place. An amazing come-back by Notts. Only a couple of months ago we trailed both Sutton and Torquay by twelve or fifteen points. We had a few games in hand and now we have pegged them back.

In the Notts County v Sutton match, the Notts fullback Kelly-Evans got himself sent off in the seventieth minute with the game at 2-2. The same Kelly-Evans that took Adam Thomas out at the knees in our fixture at Meadow Lane. It amazes me how some players lose their mind under pressure. Notts were desperate for the win being just outside the play-off spots. But the player goes into a totally rash tackle whilst already on a yellow.

Similar happened in the City v PSG Champions League semi-final the day after the Notts/ Sutton game. With City 2-0 up and in the sixty-seventh minute, Di Maria kicks out at a City player when they try to retrieve the ball off the pitch. Straight red. With another twenty-five minutes left, three goals was a tall order for PSG but there was still plenty of time left. Then, more PSG players lost the plot and received yellow cards. Teams need cool heads in crunch matches.

Fortunately, Rusk has instilled good discipline within the County team.

The omens seem good for my match completion record this season. Another social event was arranged for Saturday just gone. The mother in law's 80th birthday "do" involving a gathering of family members at our place in the afternoon/evening. Good job Dover decided to curtail their season therefore making Saturday's planned fixture void. A free Saturday perfectly co-ordinated with a family event. Otherwise, I would have been planning how to watch the match live and keep my record going of viewing every minute of every match live.

This last weekend was the tenth anniversary of our last match in the football league. On Saturday 7th May 2011 County drew 1-1 against Cheltenham at Edgeley Park. Greg Tansey scored a ninetieth minute equaliser in front of 5,000 fans. We only won nine games finishing rock bottom of League Two. 4,163 was a decent home average considering County had subjected us to several high scoring defeats at home. By the time we'd lost 1-4 at home to Macc in February I'd already resigned myself to the drop into non-league.

Even a glass half full guy like me couldn't muster the required optimism to expect a magical recovery. It was still a major shock when it actually happened. Most Hatters fans were convinced it was a case of straight back up the next season. Unfortunately, the reality was that the National Conference (as it was named then) was very similar to the bottom half of League Two. Without improving the team due to continuing financial pressure we did what was the reality. We were the bottom team in League Two and we finished sixteenth in our first season in the National Conference.

Ten years though! Ten long years that needs to come to an end soon. We have a great chance this year and three points against the Daggers will help.

Dagenham have had a great run over the last couple of months. They've won their last six matches elevating their status from just above the bottom three to just below the play-offs. This will be no easy match. Results went for us again on Saturday with Hartlepool losing 2-4 at home to Maidenhead and Torquay being held to a 0-0 draw at home to Bromley. Sutton won. With only four matches to go we still have a mathematical chance to win the league if the top two Torquay and Sutton drop points. We've already overtaken Hartlepool. Here's hoping for something close to a miracle!

It is tipping it down at Edgeley Park like on Saturday against Wealdstone. Not as windy but a steady deluge of precipitation. The pitch will be slick. Ideal for fast passing and probably some slips and mistakes. In five previous meeting we've won four and drawn one. Caldwell and Madden are upfront again with Reid on the bench. A bench that he has made a nice habit of getting off and scoring. The rain eases up for kick-off.

Youngster Rydel also starts for County replacing the injured Walker. Within five minutes it is clear that the Daggers are a quality team bang in form. They are moving the ball around at pace and are on the front foot. Their number nine McCallum looks particularly dangerous. With some relief we open the scoring on thirty-four minutes. Newby dispatches a great cross that fizzes along the six-yard line to the back post where Paddy Madden side foots the ball into the Daggers net.

This doesn't deter our visitors who keep pressing until they equalise ten minutes later. That man McCallum converts a back post header from a corner. Madden takes a knock on the ankle and is replaced by Reid at half-time. For the first twenty minutes of the second period the Daggers dominate us. They are the best team we have played this season. Bang in form, they look like a play-off outfit but they may have left it too late this season.

County are too deep for most of the second half with Dagenham the better team. Our visitors hit the bar and have two good penalty shouts turned down. The impressive Rydel is replaced with Bennett on seventy-seven minutes.

We have three strikers on the pitch now as we go for a winner. A winner that would keep us in the hunt for top spot. Dagenham looked like they should have had a pen in the ninety-second minute which would have left us with no points from the match.

The game ends all square as County extend their unbeaten run to fifteen matches. Possibly the best team we have played all season, the Daggers will consider themselves a tad unlucky not to leave with three points. The impressive Rydel was man of the match. Sutton won 3-2 at home to Woking.

Barring a miracle, tonight's draw sees the end of our title challenge. It looks like second or third place for us now meaning we would get a home tie in the play-off semi-finals. If victorious, we would then play the final at Ashton Gate, home of Bristol City.

Sunday May 16th 2021

County 2 v Torquay United 2

Way back on the 3rd October 2020 in Chapter Ten I reported on the first league match of the season away at Torquay. Will we rue our luck that day? We battered The Gulls but left Devon with nil points after a single goal defeat. Much the better side, the Torquay commentators described our pressure on their goal as like the siege of the Alamo. However, the Gulls just kept on improving after that game opening up a big lead at the top of the table by January. The turn of the year saw a dip in form allowing Sutton to occupy top spot.

The importance of the game has elevated this clash to the BT live match choice of the weekend. 12:15pm kick off and a switch to Sunday. There is a show of support from the County faithful from 11am on Hardcastle Road outside the mecca of English football, Edgeley Park. This is to make sure the players can hear and see the fans to provide that "twelfth man" boost. The fans aren't allowed inside until next Saturday.

This season seems to be panning out perfectly considering the force majeure that occurred. I've already mentioned two potential fixture clashes with family events. Both averted thankfully. One when I watched Alty away on Boxing Day while entertaining the extended family. They basically sympathised with my obsession. Secondly, as we hosted the mother in laws 80th when we should have been playing Dover away. It wasn't a problem as Dover had already thrown in the towel meaning the fixture was "voided."

The next dilemma is the timing of the play-off semi-finals and potential final. We have a weekend with another couple planned at a hotel in the Lakes in June. Organised by my better half and my mates better half. Their priorities are for a post pandemic treat. A bit of luxury. They certainly weren't checking for County's potential play-off match dates. It has been announced that our potential play-off final at Ashton Gate will be on the 20th June. With some trepidation, I checked when our Lakes sojourn was taking place. Luckily, it was for the following weekend.

With a fair bit of relief, I announced to the missus and Jonnie that we are all going to Bristol! Jonnie and I will attend a potential play-off final during a weekend break in cider country. The missus can chill out for a few hours while we are at the match. I'll even try to get an extra ticket, if possible, for Kath! I spent five minutes expounding the virtues of the capital of the southwest. With work I went to Xmas "dos" with clients for several years in "Brizzol". That involved night spots and clubs and very late finishes! I am sure that I can find some cultural locations to visit too. Hotel is booked.

To today's game, what are the permutations to decide the title winners? Considering it is between Sutton, Torquay, with us and Hartlepool as outsiders, let's start with today's visitors. We have three matches to go and we are five points behind the Gulls. Win today and we are two points behind with two games left. Seeing as we have a much better goal difference, we would then need to win our last two matches and Torquay would need to get four points or less and we would usurp them.

Sutton- beat Maidenhead 3-0 away yesterday. Barring bottling it in the last two games, Sutton have won it. Now nine points behind with a game in hand and with a similar goal difference, County would need to win all three and Sutton lose their last two games.

Hartlepool- beat Aldershot away 3-1 yesterday. Pools leapfrog us into third place. We are one point behind them with a game in hand.

It looks like Sutton have won the league.

I dropped Jonnie off at his fixture in Bolton. I normally watch his games but he will get back after kick-off for the Torquay match. Kath is away, so I've organised a lift back for Jonnie. I swung by EP to check out the pre-match fans sing-song in support of the team. Some good chants and a few flares. I left to get back for the 12 o'clock start for the coverage by BT. Only a ten-minute drive so easy for me. BT have Chris Hargreaves as the on-pitch co-presenter. Chris who? He made 131 appearances for Torquay.

The sun is shining and the Railway End is resplendent with its new seats now spelling out the letters COUNTY in white. The cherry on the Railway End cake is the now unfurled new scoreboard. An impressive TV screen type structure.

Torquay need three points to stay in the title chase. We need three points to stay in the race for a top three place and that all important one-off home tie in the playoff semi-finals.

The Gulls enter the pitch in their white away shirts. They could have worn their traditional yellow but as per modern football parlance it seems standard for teams to use any opportunity to promote their change strips. Recalling my visit to Plainmoor when on holiday in 1977, Torquay did wear white at the time in a temporary change from yellow. As did County who wore white shirts for most of the 70's before reverting to blue.

Madden will be out for "a few weeks" after receiving that knock on his ankle in the last match against The Daggers. The opening exchanges see Newby linking up well with Cardwell. For the Gulls, Wynter down the right, Little and Randell look particularly dangerous. On fourteen minutes a brilliant move sees Southam-Hales and Cardwell exchange a slick one-two before Reid delivers a great shot. The Brazilian keeper Lucas, thwarts Reid. On the half hour Southam-Hales curls an excellent shot from the corner of the eighteen-yard box which eludes Lucas to put County ahead.

After the co-commentator describes Torquay's assistant manager as one of football's Mr Nice guys, he gets sent off. Aaron Davies took exception to a throw-in decision just before our goal and proceeded to provide the referee and fourth official with a barrage of expletives. Mr Davies was duly dispatched to the stands.

Our lead lasts only five minutes when after concerted pressure Croasdale over-stretches and trips a Torquay player in the box. Boden strikes the penalty with power right down the middle for 1-1. County started the second half in the ascendancy, creating chances and playing slick football. Against the run of play Torquay took the lead in the fifty-second minute with a scruffy goal. Boden completed his brace in the match after converting his own flick which rebounded off the crossbar.

The score was brought level again when Ash Palmer converted a trademark back post header from a Rooney corner eight minutes later. A great header making it a creditable six goals for the season. In the last fifteen minutes Torquay brought on their big defender Cameron and stuck him upfront. Their policy was to go long in search of the winner. County finished the match well but the deadlock could not be broken.

The point puts us ahead of Hartlepool on goal difference. We just need to match or better Pools in the last two matches to secure third place as our goal difference is far superior.

Sutton play Hartlepool at home next Saturday which will be difficult for Pools. Sutton have pretty much won the league now.

One of the best if not the best match of the season. Two really good teams battled away for ninety minutes. A great advertisement for the National League on national telly. Both teams would more than hold their own in League Two.

Saturday May 22nd 2021

County 1 v Woking 1

It was my birthday yesterday. Amazingly I am fifty-four years old. I look younger (so say some) and I certainly feel pretty much the same as when I was thirty. Or younger. In fact, I feel pretty much the same as when I was eighteen. Back then I was football and music mad. I still am. I've got married and helped raise three kids but I'm that same guy as back in the 80's or 90's to all intent and purposes.

That's how life works. It goes by pretty quick but you can assess what's gone before. Footy and music is good at putting the decades into perspective. The teams or rock albums that you can pinpoint back to the 80's, 90's or 2000's provide memories. You remember all the things you've done or seen.

So, what would be an amazing birthday present? Considering what has gone before in the last twelve months, attending a football match inside Edgeley Park is about as good as it gets. Today is the day that fans have been counting down to. The first match that we can attend in over twelve months. I did actually attend two pre-season matches. One by ticket and one by blag (the only County fan at Guiseley). But this is the real thing today, a league match with three valuable points at stake.

This has been a mad season with all the pandemic malarkey. If you are reading this all I can say is thank you. It started out as a mission to attend as many matches as possible then the virus struck. By the end of the summer it looked perfectly feasible that fans might be back in by October/

November. We then got a massive second wave that shut the country back down over Xmas. This scuppered any real chance of getting back into Edgeley Park. Some areas had a short reprieve if they were located in tier two. Some fans got back in. County even played in front of fans at Bromley in December 2020.

So the day has come. We tread the terraces of our second home once again. Who would have thought it would be the last home game of the season before we could attend a County match. Going back to the start of the book and my recollections of the Tranmere match in 1986, I will feel a similar emotional pull walking down Hardcastle Road. Absence from the stadium has made the heart grow fonder. With all the ground improvements, it will be extra special to get back inside Edgeley Park. In fact, with the takeover, investment and the team on the cusp of the play-offs I may have to pinch myself to check it isn't all a dream.

Maybe I'll wake up and realise that we are still a cash strapped semi-professional team with an uncertain future. Thankfully, it is reality and this fifty-four-year-old bloke is full of a child like excitement. The beauty being that I can share it today with my sixteen-year-old son. It is extra special as Jonnie has never really seen County in all its pomp. His whole life has seen a steady decline with a very recent upturn in the team's fortunes. Maybe, I can complete a full County conversion of him!

This week has been a week of consistent precipitation again. After a record dry April our meteorological luck has changed making May a potentially record damp month. We are used to it of course in the beautiful northwest of England. Fortunately, my weather app indicates a dry day today. Good job as our temporary season tickets are located in the shiny new seats in the uncovered Railway End. Due to the social distancing required we have been bumped along into our temporary location. Even Cheadle Enders have been bumped right around to the Railway End.

County are being very conscientious with their covid regime. Rightly so but looking at some of the Premier League matches with reduced crowds there doesn't seem to have been the same rigour. At Chelsea the other night, the fans seemed bunched together en masse. Today we are temperature tested and have staggered arrival times starting at 1pm. Fortunately, our slot is for a 2pm arrival. That is fine for me as it gives us an hour to absorb the feeling of being in the ground again and appreciate the recent stadium works. Good job it's not raining though!

We arrive at the stadium bob on time and enter the Railway End finding our seats located on the edge of the new U in the COUNTY letters. Just under the impressive new scoreboard eight rows up. Everyone is well spaced out in their groups. You could get many more in and still maintain social distancing. Martin Tyler is stood in front of us directing Woking's warm-up. I didn't realise he is part of their set up.

The players are met with loud claps and cheers as they enter the pitch. It is brilliant to be back and the hour we had to wait flew by as we soaked up our surroundings after over a year away. I fully expected a victory against a team who have lost their last ten matches. Unexpectedly, the Cards haven't folded as they put up stubborn resistance.

We have gone with Reid upfront on his own, surprisingly. Rooney is playing a deep quarter back role. Southam-Hales is having plenty of joy down the wing but Tom Walker is being a bit wasteful. The result being that we are getting balls into the box but nobody is in the danger zone. Either Reid is in the wrong area or the cross is delivered to the wrong space.

Combine this with Woking having joy on the break and we start to have some jitters. The Cards have won their previous three visits, so maybe they are a bogie side. On forty-four minutes Woking took the lead when a free kick ricocheted around the box before being poked home by Kretzschmar. From our low angle at the other end it was hard to see properly. To our relief within two minutes we equalised on half time when a Rooney shot hit the post, Reid re-directed from a tight angle before their big centre half deflected into his own net. We got an amazing close-up view in front of us. But overall it made me hanker for my usual seats in the middle of the Pop Side where you get a full view of the pitch and the action.

Second half we could only improve on the lack-lustre first period and we did. We were camped in their half. At one point it was nearly fifteen minutes without the Cards crossing the half-way line. Bennett came on to add fire power in the box. We hit the bar twice, had fifteen corners overall and it looked like we had a couple cleared off the line. Being at the other end of the pitch it was hard to see the action properly from our angle. We just couldn't score. Woking played as if they needed the point to stay up which they didn't. They wasted time, rolled around on the ground and were a general pain in the arse.

All square on our return to Edgeley Park. Plenty of effort but ultimately a disappointing one point. We could have done with three just in case Hartlepool provide a shock away at Sutton. If Hartlepool win then it is in their hands for third spot.

What a great day. The whole ritual of travelling to the game, walking the usual route to the ground, chats with other fans and watching the game in familiar surroundings was cathartic. I could tell Jonnie was buzzing too. His appreciation for Southam-Hales and his antipathy for Bennett was still there. Everyone has their favourites! It is all about opinions. Usually with a gallows humour.

The players were fully aware of the fans. The Cards goalie Ross tweeted about it being good to have ninety minutes of abuse. It was partly self-inflicted as he did seem to time waste from the first minute. He got mostly humorous jibes. We are back and it feels good.

Sutton beat the Monkey Hangers 3-0 securing the title. Worthy champs they did us a favour. Now Pools are one point behind us with one game left. We have a fifteen better goal difference. If we lose at Yeovil and Pools only draw at home to Weymouth, we finish third. If they win, we have to win. Basically we need to go for the win at Huish Park!

Saturday May 29th 2021
Yeovil 0 v County 1

Earlier in the book you may recall me mentioning Yeovil in the context of long distance away travels and the varying degrees of enjoyment. Ranging from the ecstasy of a League Cup victory at Southampton in 96/97 to the boredom of a run of the mill away draw at Yeovil and a painfully long journey home. The type of match whereby you decide to never return to Yeovil. But once the team returns to form, you forget all about the experience and repeat the journey.

Today we play The Glovers of Yeovil at Huish Park in Somerset. Last week was the first time County fans could be at the match in more than spirit as the official return of fans happened for the Woking home match. Unfortunately, away fans are still not allowed in at Yeovil today. If we could have won the league today, I would have gone and somehow tried to sneak a view into the match and potentially celebrate promotion. However, we are resigned to the play-offs and fans are allowed to attend the play-off semi-final and potential final.

The draw of match attendance is something that becomes almost like a fever to some fans. They have to be there. Back in the last millennium as a youngster I read the book The Loneliness of the Long-Distance Runner. A tale of a teenager who takes up running to escape his mundane working-class life. Typically for a football fan, I started out working in a mill doing a mundane job. Cutting cloth for Ron Hill Sports.

Ron was the famous Commonwealth gold-medallist runner born in Accrington and living in Hyde where he had his factory producing runners clothing. Ron ran every day for over fifty years. He passed away this week and received obituaries from around the world. Ron was a legend of long-distance and marathon running.

The cutting bit in Ron's mill was OK but the laying of endless layers of cloth was mundane toil. Humour got you through. The radio, Mickey taking and football chat helped. By the end of the week I was always looking forward to going to the match. Not going would leave a hollow feeling usually filled with going to the pub. Footy is/was very important to the working class.

Thirty odd years later I am now a member of the bourgeois. After all, I couldn't lay cloth forever and these kids cost a lot of dosh. To further annoy any Marxists out there, I now drive an Audi. But I do have the Royal Enfield motorbike. Today though, rather than travelling south to Dorset we are travelling north to see our eldest son in Newcastle who is at Northumberland Uni.

If we could have been promoted today, I would have been in Huish Park. Somehow, I would have blagged in. I did apply for Yeovil tickets. Their website required registration with their ticket agency. I signed up using my brother in laws details in London with the theory that an exiled Glover in London would look significantly less suspicious than an exiled Glover in Stockport! It appeared to say that tickets were available but kept bumping me off. Maybe it identified my IP address which set off a blagger alarm!

To today's match where the garment themed Glovers host the Hatters. I am watching on my phone. If you recall I did the same for the Kidderminster pre-season match when visiting eldest son Will up in Newcastle. We are in fact at the beach. Yes, they do of course have beaches near Newcastle. We are on a trip out to Tynemouth. Nice place too with a castle and a priory overlooking an impressive bay. The weather is pretty nippy temperature wise even though it is late May.

Will informed me that 20 degrees C would be considered a heat wave up here. In Newcastle it is 21 degrees C. But just eight miles east on the coast it is misty and several degrees cooler. You can hear ship horns out in the mist, signalling each other to prevent collisions in the pea-souper fog.

The match has an early kick-off at 12:30. There is the Championship play-off final at three and the Champions League final at eight. Then the Euro's start in two weeks with County in the play-off final in three weeks (hopefully). One thing is for sure, we need three points today presuming that Hartlepool defeat lowly Weymouth at home. County have lost just one of ten previous meetings with Yeovil and are unbeaten in all our previous visits to Huish Park – the last of which came in August 2019, where an Adam Thomas goal salvaged a 1-1 draw.

I hope I haven't tempted fate by quoting those stats. The camera stream is at a flat distant angle exacerbated by the fact I am watching on my phone. To be honest, I am not getting massive value for the £9.99 I have shelled out by the footy on show either. However, the excitement of the action is almost secondary today. This match could be the most boring match ever but if we win, we will secure the all-important third spot. That is sort of how it panned out, fortunately. County controlled the game, scored the one goal required and professionally played the game out.

Pre-kick-off, there was a nice dedication to Lee Collins the Glovers captain who passed away earlier in the season. Yeovil kept the game competitive even though they had a multitude of loan players playing their last game and several injured players out. The game was decided by John Rooney's twenty first goal of the season. A deflected shot mid-way through the first half. A sixth straight away win for Rusk's men sets up a National League play-off semi-final at Edgeley Park, against the victors of Hartlepool United vs Bromley.

Job done, all that was left to do was sit in the sun back in Jesmond with the missus and the two lads enjoying a few celebratory lagers. I can highly recommend Tynemouth and one of my regular haunts over the years- Jesmond in Newcastle. It is a bank holiday weekend; the sun is shining and the lager is cold. Life couldn't get much better.

To cap it off, County have made a nice gesture in announcing they won't be charging season ticket holders for the play-off semi-final. This season has been full of trials and tribulations. After shelling out for season tickets without knowing when we would get back in the ground, fans showed loyalty. We all thought we would be back in the ground pretty quickly. As it happened, it wasn't until the last home match of the season until we entered Edgeley Park. Fortunately, the fans have seen County put a massive shift in that has resulted in a play-off semi-final.

CHAPTER EIGHTEEN
June 2021

The qualifying (quarter final) play-off results update...

Here we are in the merry month of June. Summer has arrived. Folk are out in the sun drinking and eating boosting the economy back to normality. Tis a season to be jolly.

We have the European Championships and County in the play-offs. Life is good, if not a tad nervy as I watch the play-off qualifiers (or quarter-finals). I am confident in the boys but it's all getting serious now.

Notts County beat Chesterfield 3-2 to play Torquay in the semi-final. A great match. Ex County player Danny Rowe scored a scorcher for Chesterfield.

A free kick. I immediately worried that Danny is going to come back to haunt us. Notts won out in the end with both teams looking like a stern test if we should play them. One consolation was that the Chesterfield goals involved average to poor defending offering a chink in the Notts armour.

In the other quarter-final at Hartlepool, Bromley didn't show up in the first half as the Monkey Hangers stuck three past them with no reply.

Helped by poor defending in the first half, Pools then allowed the Lillywhites back into the game with the score ending up 3-2. So we play Pools at high noon next Sunday. Meanwhile at the same time, Torquay host Notts County.

This is it, the business end of the season. Crunch time, squeaky bum time, whatever you want to call it.

Sunday June 13th 2021 – Play-off Semi Final
County 0 v Hartlepool 1

Hopefully, this is the penultimate match of the season. County have home advantage with the best unbeaten streak in the league coming into this match. Our beloved Hatters are in good shape. I am approaching this one with a positive attitude. May the best team win and all that. If we fall at this hurdle, we have had a very good season. All looks well for another go at winning it next season if we should lose today with the club in excellent shape from top to bottom.

Win it today and the nerves will continue to jangle into the final at Bristol City next Sunday. Today, Jonnie and I are undercover in the Together Stand previously known as the Barlow Stand or the Pop Side. Social distancing has been relaxed a little bit further with around 2,700 fans allowed in. An increase on the 2,200 for the Woking game. The club have kindly provided free tickets to season ticket holders. A thanks for our loyalty this season having viewed all but one match via the streams.

Season Ticket renewals started last week with over 1,000 sold in the first week. Optimism is high amongst the ranks of the County faithful. We have renewed with prices frozen again meaning good value for the National League and excellent value for League Two (if we get promoted). Today is an early kick off at high noon as England play Croatia at 2pm in their first match of the European Championships. Fingers and toes crossed for a Hatters/ Three Lions double victory.

I suppose a noon kick off is better for the nerves as waiting until three prolongs the anticipation to a fever pitch. Let's get it on. We know who we could play next week now too. I watched the other semi yesterday from Plainmoor. Great atmosphere as per the Notts v Chesterfield quarter-final last week. These really are great matches. The fans are so glad to be back in the grounds that the atmosphere seems even better than expected. You don't notice the below capacity covid crowds either. It is almost as if the chants are more joyous.

Full credit to the Torquay fans chants. They have a drum which is OK even though I'm not a massive fan of poorly syncopated rhythms. The constant sound of scrunching crisp packets is in fact standard issue plastic clappers. That most annoying of modern sports crowd accessories. They should be banned at football matches. We are an established sport with traditional crowd etiquette. Happy clappers are more for American sports or maybe hockey or athletics. It creates a noise but one that annoys me. Call me an old git but I prefer old school noise.

These matches have so much jeopardy on them they are a compelling watch. Probably impacted by the fact my team are involved in the scenario. Having said that I can accept the jeopardy of defeat. We've progressed this season and if we should start next season in the National League the club is still on the up. I am convincing myself that this is the best mind-set!

The victors were Torquay. 2-2 after normal time. They scored a third in the first period of extra time quickly followed by a dubious penalty. Notts came back straight away but were thwarted by a great save and then the crossbar. 4-2 at the end. Notts were unlucky with the pen but the Gulls edged it.

Torquay progress to the final. They've spent seven years out of the football league including a spell in the National League South. This is the non-league Bermuda Triangle. Ex-league teams have disappeared under mysterious circumstances into this void. Notts have been down here for two years. Last year they reached the final and now they've lost in the semi-final. Their fans must realise that no matter how big the club, there is no guaranteed navigation out of the situation. We have spent a decade down here while Wrexham have been here for twelve years.

We are in the Pop Side as I still like to refer to the Together stand. Noon kick off and we have a perfectly timed 11:15 arrival slot to meet covid condition rules. I'll be glad when

I hear the back of that term. Speaking of back, at least the Pop Side now has a back. As I mentioned earlier in this blog, back in the 80's there was a massive gap in the back of the stand through which wind would hit the backs of the beleaguered supporters stood on the terraces. The stand had been reduced in size in the 70's and the back wall was only built halfway up making the experience of watching County even more frustrating in our Fourth Division Days. Especially in winter.

Today we don't need to worry about wind or cold. It is lovely shirt sleeve weather or even shorts. In fact, I am wearing shorts it's that warm and my '67 Fourth Division Championship retro shirt. It was lucky earlier in the season so it's back. I'm going to hope County win but yesterday put sport back into perspective. Christian Eriksen collapsed on the pitch playing for Denmark in the Euro's receiving CPR before being stabilised in the changing rooms.

The Monkey Hangers don their yellow away kit for the match. County jog on and there is a raucous welcome from all sides. No away fans of course so there are Hatters fans on all four sides. We are going to be the twelfth man win or lose. I am feeling nervous now. In fact after a week of mild confidence, I started to "brick it" in the car driving to the match.

Madden has benefited from a full week of training after a spell out with injury. Up front is Cardwell. Rooney has just won the National League player of the year for the second time running. We are sat near the TV gantry that has a sign on the back requesting no swearing. Good look with that. Located in this section is a vocal group of loyal supporters including Mozzer, a well-known fan. The chants are always humorous but I can't guarantee no swearing.

County huff and puff in the first half. Pools look solid but we have the only chances. Madden skewed one wide early on. The new scoreboard is now playing video as promised. A compilation of County fans sending Come on County messages is played through the screen and speakers before the match. County goalkeeping legend Alan Ogley takes over the microphone pre-match and urges the crowd to "rattle and roll" and get behind the lads.

At half time I ventured away from my recent healthy diet drive by sampling one of our new pies. County have employed the Great North Pie Company as pie supplier. In a bid to enhance the match going experience the club have veered away from the perfunctory Hollands pie offer. Although I can enthusiastically eat a Hollands pie, if you are going to pay over the odds for one in a football ground you might as well have a cordon bleu version.

The second half follows the same pattern. County are "rattling" but not really "rolling". The Monkey Hangers have more possession but hardly a shot on goal. Rooney goes close forcing a good save. Newby comes on followed by Reid. We look a bit scruffy on the ball, then on seventy minutes Pools get a scruffy goal. A speculative shot from just outside the box takes a slight deflection. Hinchliffe gets his fingertips to it but it sneaks into the net just inside the post. I am now getting very twitchy. I don't feel like we've done enough. Even with twenty minutes to go it feels like we're not going to score.

Bennett comes on in the last ten minutes and has one chance. Richie did well with a header but the keeper bundled it away. The game sort of fades out. Credit to Pools as they are solid as a unit. Madden and Rooney huffed and puffed. Hogan and Palmer have played great at the back. We just didn't have enough going forward to break down the resolute opposition. In a tight game we edged it three to one on good chances. The Monkey Hangers scored theirs.

The fans drift away at the final whistle. Mozzer and his crew blast out a defiant rendition of The Scarf as the ref blows the whistle on our season. We'll be back next year for another go at getting out of non-league.

There was a sombre mood but before we got back to the car, I had cheered myself up. This is County after all. It's not supposed to be an easy ride.

Back home I cracked open an ice-cold beer and put the England game on. At half time I cancelled my Bristol hotel. My glass is still half full. I filled it with more beer. We are still in non-league but I have enjoyed the season all in all. We'll be OK. The club is in a better place now. News comes through of another result. My daughter just got a first at Glasgow Uni. A magnificent result. Some consolation and probably the most important result to be fair. The best result!

But I'll still be there next year at some non-league outpost. It's in the blood. When this team has gone and another comes to the fore. When the manager is replaced, we'll still be here. In victory, in defeat it's what we do. The eccentrics, the young recruits, the certified, the addicted. It's what makes football unique.

It's just another day in the life of a lower league football fan. Oh, and England have just scored!

EPILOGUE

The 2020/2021 football season has to be the most tumultuous campaign in the history of the game. In fact, outside world wars this year was the most tumultuous year in the history of the UK and possibly the world in general. We had force majeure in the form of the pandemic resulting in the lockdown of society. Freedoms were restricted in the UK like never seen before. Even in the blitz of the second world war, people had more freedom of movement. The pubs even stayed open during the blitz. Football was suspended of course due to lack of players who were serving in the forces. When the players returned the league's restarted with the same teams.

2020/2021 was different. We had the season suspended and play-off positions decided on points per game. Macclesfield and Bury went bust. Both had other financial transgressions but covid would have seen them off. Overall financial pressures on clubs intensified as revenue streams dried up. The financial tight rope had been shaken. With most clubs living beyond their means, the unthinkable scenario of the suspension of fixtures and a further entire season without fan revenue became reality. The fall out is likely to threaten the existence of more clubs into the 2021/2022 season. Stockport County would have been under threat too. Fortunately, the takeover in early 2020 protected us from potential financial crisis.

For the Hatters, the new regime took over the operations behind the scenes commercially and in the coaching set up. We appointed a Director of Football and a team of new coaches. Several new players were recruited. Results went well and we progressed to the FA Cup third round, playing West Ham. Then sitting joint third in the league in January, Jim Gannon was sacked. After a thousand games as a player and manager Jim was relieved of his duties as he didn't fit into the new "culture" at the club.

An unknown young coach was appointed. After initial bumps in the road the team was galvanised under new manager Simon Rusk. The country stabilised the covid crisis with an efficient vaccination programme.

The loss of revenue for the super-rich owners of the "elite" European clubs caused by the pandemic led to the cynical creation of a European Super League. Another threat to our cherished pyramid. If successful, the ESL would have been catastrophic for the financial set up of the pyramid effectively constricting the ambitions of all clubs.

Fortunately, the idea was rejected, filed away as one of the monumentally bad ideas in football history.

In the end, at the very end of a bizarre season, order was finally restored and fans returned to grounds for the final matches. County had supporters in Edgeley Park for the first time for the final home match of the regular season.

With all the turmoil and upheaval it was with some relief that County navigated themselves to the play-off semi-finals by finishing third in the league. An excellent performance by the manager and squad. The new investment didn't necessarily guarantee a top three finish in the first season. Having to play in behind closed doors conditions, the new squad put a massive shift in to achieve third spot.

However, the curse of the lower league football fan or fans of most teams transpired. After all the effort, County lost in the semi-finals and we were consigned to another season in non-league. Being favourites going into the match made no difference.

This is County after all, and we like to do things the hard way. Hartlepool overcame us and go to Bristol for the final. Hotels cancelled I had a beer. If I can take what has happened to us over the last decade (or most of our history), I can take this.

I'll be back again next season supporting the Hatters. I've come this far so I can't stop now.

COME ON THE COUNTY BOYS!

Thank you for reading this blog. Before I get too emotional, I'm signing off. Stay safe. I'm getting another beer (and another tissue). Cheers, Stew.

ACKNOWLEDGEMENTS

Big Thanks to the following for inspiration and assistance-

My Granddad- Even though he was a staunch Red, he took me to my first County match in 1975 when I was eight.

Victor Publishing- Thanks Merv for publishing the book and all your help

Stuart Crawford- For donating his amazing personal scrap books of County seasons from the 80s & 90s

Martin Frost - for his amazing recollections of watching County at 57hattersyears.co.uk

Jon Keighren, Phil Brennan, Dave Espley and other County fans- for inspiration and mutual enthusiasm for County!

The Scarf Bergara Wore Podcast- great stuff from the lads on there

Akito Aoki - The Tokyo Hatter. Amazing enthusiasm from the other side of the world!

Other book inspirations -Friday Night Is County Night, Vintage Port, Saturday Night and Thursday Morning and all the great History and A-Z County books

For helping me get into the match (or try to get in)!-

Stockport County ticket office

Trudi Hannaford - Guiseley FC (an innocent blag that was met with friendly assistance)

Graham Watkinson- Chorley FC (the match was cancelled but Graham kindly arranged a press pass)

Torquay, Halifax, Wealdstone etc (thank you for the kind responses to my requests to try to get into matches)

Printed in Great Britain
by Amazon